150 YEARS OF WESTERN ART
PAINTING SCULPTURE ARCHITECTURE

The neoclassicists' exciting search for the spirit of classical art... the development of the great Paris Salon of 1824 which paved the way to Romanticism... the Realists' fight for the lone painter's survival... the violent emotional outburst of the Fauvists and the Cubist's counter-movement... the jarring world of abstract expressionism... the dazzling achievement of modern architecture.

ART IN THE MODERN WORLD
A sweeping history of the major art movements
of the modern world

Art historian Norman Schlenoff is Professor of Humanities at City University of New York. He has studied at the Fogg Museum of Harvard University and at the Institute of Fine Arts of New York University. He received a *Docteur ès-Lettres* from the Sorbonne. Recipient of a Guggenheim Fellowship for research in nineteenth-century French art, Professor Schlenoff is the author of *Romanticism and Realism in Painting* and two books on Ingres.

ART IN THE MODERN WORLD

For Althea

BANTAM MATRIX EDITIONS

art in the
modern world

·

by Norman Schlenoff
Professor of Humanities
City University of New York

·

BANTAM BOOKS
NEW YORK / TORONTO / LONDON

ART IN THE MODERN WORLD
Bantam Matrix edition / published November 1965

Library of Congress Catalog Card Number: 65-26247

Published simultaneously in the United States and Canada

Bantam Books are published by Bantam Books, Inc., a subsidiary
of Grosset & Dunlap, Inc. Its trade-mark, consisting of the words
"Bantam Books" and the portrayal of a bantam, is registered in the
United States Patent Office and in other countries. Marca Registrada.
Bantam Books, Inc., 271 Madison Avenue, New York, N.Y. 10016.

PRINTED IN THE UNITED STATES OF AMERICA

CONTENTS

1
NEOCLASSICISM
1800–1825

David: *Portrait of Madame Récamier*.
1800. Louvre, Paris. (Arch. Photo)

■ In the beginning of the nineteenth century a Greek and Roman vocabulary of learning was translated into the languages of European nations. The mode affected every corner of living, not only painting, sculpture, and architecture, but also fashion in dress and manners, ideas—and literature, where the ancient themes, translated and imitated, enjoyed a great vogue. The ancient world became the model for emulation; ethics and laws were patterned on the past and contemporary culture was an obedient disciple too. Impetus was given to the trend by the excavations of such cities as Pompeii, and publications of the antiquities of Athens by Stuart and Revett, among others. The classic revival was far-reaching; even in the United States the old Republican Roman laws and the Greek arts and virtues were admired. In the arts this new interest in the ancient world fostered a Neoclassicism which, archeological in spirit, reinterpreted classical antiquity by modeling itself directly on ancient examples in art and architecture.

The aspiring artist who came to the Paris of 1800 was immediately aware of the leadership of the great Jacques Louis David (1748-1825). Colossus astride two centuries, David, at that time working on his portrait of Madame Récamier, had already passed through several styles. A few years before the great revolution of 1789 he had been attracted, in his *Mars and Venus,* to the Rococo style of his famous cousin François Boucher.

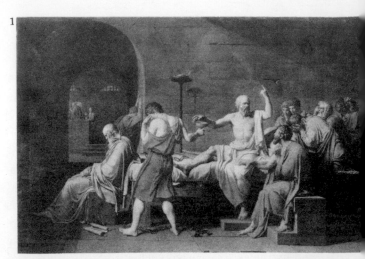

1. David: *Death of Socrates*. 1787.
Metropolitan Museum of Art, New York.

2. David: *The Sabines*. 1799.
Louvre, Paris. (Arch. Photo)

The Rococo, with its restless small opposing movements over the surface of the canvas creating intricate curvilinear decorative patterns in pretty colors and soft surfaces, emphasized the sensuous and erotic, the charming and indolent world of pleasure. In 1775 David visited Rome; there he was influenced by his Neoclassicist teacher Vien and by classical antiquity; he absorbed as a matter of course the Italian Renaissance and the French classical tradition of seventeenth-century Poussin. David changed his style, and in such paintings as the *Death of Socrates* of 1787 presented an ancient theme in Neoclassical setting; and along with this change, a new persuasive moral sense fortified his story of the persevering philosopher dying for truth. Because of his moralizing force David emerged as a spokesman for the French Revolution of 1789, painting the *Death of Marat* in 1793 to commemorate the martyrdom of one of the leaders. There he shows his admiration for early Baroque style—the opposition of light and form, each related to and independent of the other in the same way as are two themes in a Bach fugue.

The aspiring young artist of 1800 would then begin to absorb France as France was to absorb him. In the eighteenth century, French culture had asserted itself and spread all over the Continent; afterward, French dominance in the arts continued through the nine-

1

1. David: *Death of Marat*. 1793. Brussels
Royal Museum of Fine Arts. (Photo Bulloz)

2. David: *Madame Daru*. 1810. Frick Museum,
Copyright: the Frick Collection, New York.

teenth century and into the next. Paris was congenial soil for the young artist, who retained his nationality while he gallicized his spirit. Since 1800 France has functioned in just that way, siphoning off all that is best in the rest of the Western world to strain it through the sieve of a Gallic outlook, mixing elements from everywhere to select what is most pertinent to the construction of a work of art. It is for this reason that France, the focus of cultural vitality, will play so important a part in the history of art in the two centuries that are spread out before us.

Animated, then, by the achievement of the Romans, David began to move colored marble statues—so writer Madame de Staël complained—like pieces on a chessboard against a severe and flat decor. In his *Death of Socrates* the solid sculptural bodies are stressed in a row of figures moving across a proscenium; the clear rectangular space of the painting is monotonously severe. In style and theme David set a pattern for others. A great painter, he was able to redefine classicism through his own talent, so that men thereafter spoke of the Davidians and Davidianism.

In 1797 David suddenly changed to a "Greek" style. The myth of the perfection of the Greek world was in the air. Napoleon's treaties had brought to Paris great numbers of ancient art works; artists were able now to re-evaluate their notions of the past, now to grasp direct the ancient manner, without the overlay of Renaissance and Baroque interpretations through which they had previously seen it. Young artists in David's studio vaunted the new theories everywhere, gathering to discuss their plan of action. One group, known as the Primitives or Bearded Ones because they

Ingres: *Madame Rivière*. 1805.
Louvre, Paris. (Arch. Photo)

1. Overbeck: *Joseph Sold by His Brother*. 1816.
National Gallery, Berlin. (Bildarchiv Foto Marburg)

2. Ingres: *Venus Wounded by Diomedes*. 1803.
Private Collection. (Photo Bulloz)

wore beards and liked very old things, felt that David's
style was Rococo and not severe enough; the Renaissance tradition, and Raphael in particular, they thought
hackneyed and a spurious reinterpretation of the ancient manner. Greece was not far enough back: one
must go further into the past, to the Old Testament
and to such heroes as Ossian (a supposed ancient
Gaelic bard) for inspiration. Unwashed and unshaved,
dressed as Greeks or undressed as Primitives, they held
orgiastic dances in the park—where in 1803 they were
at last arrested and forced to shave. With the lather
the movement came to an end—or rather, it ostensibly
came to an end; in actuality this was but a first appearance of an attitude in art that keeps cropping up all
through the century and even in our time. Since these
young men hated Raphael, they affirmed the superiority of pre-Raphaelite, Quattrocento (fifteenth-cen-
tury) and naive painting. They disliked shadows for
destroying the flat surfaces of the painting; they
scorned color for interfering with the severe and imposing lines of their nobly inspired world, where nude
and unencumbered figures might become awe-inspiring
new Moses and Jupiter images. Spurning color and
shading as illusionistic devices, they were led to a consciousness of the decorative surface of the painting, a
flattening of the picture space; and by canceling details they heightened the picture's monumentality and

Gros: *Pesthouse of Jaffa.* 1804.
Louvre, Paris. (Arch. Photo)

independence from the world of real objects. In their anti-painting attitude they gave painting a new freedom and another direction.

The *Sabines* of 1799 shows David's interest in this new movement, but it was difficult for him to depart too far from the solid sculptural monumentality of his figures. Jean Auguste Dominique Ingres (1780-1867), one of the most important of David's students, incorporated some of the Primitive elements in his *Venus Wounded by Diomedes* and his portraits of Madame Rivière of 1805 and Madame Leblanc of 1823: shadows are so reduced that any movement into the pic-

Girodet: *Ossian Welcoming Napoleonic Heroes.*
1802. Chateau de Malmaison. (Arch. Photo)

ture space is minimized, while the slight shading over
the fragile skin flattens out the features; the sharp
silhouette of the figure is increased by setting it boldly
yet carefully against a negative background whose
function it is to assert the figure and to isolate it; subtly
arranged patterns of arms and garments heighten the
decorative quality, while small opposed details set off
the monumentality of the human form. Everything is
done to enhance the integrity of the figure, the linear
boundaries circumscribing it and the full face giving
us an inviolable and placid image. All motion too
seems to be drained out of the canvas as the figure,

beyond the menace of time, calmly asserts itself in an almost pulseless world.

Contemporaries of the Primitives, a German group called the Nazarenes, immersed themselves deeply in what they hoped would be fructifying religiosity, attempting to capture the spirit of the doctrine and not merely the letter; converted Catholics, they lived and worked together in a monastery in Rome. Peter Cornelius (1783-1867), Frederic Overbeck (1789-1869), Philip Veit (1793-1877), and Wilhelm Schadow (1789-1862) collaborated in 1816 on Old Testament scenes of the history of Joseph for their Jewish patron Bartholdy; later Julius Schnorr von Carolsfeld and others joined this group. Pre-Raphaelists too, they admired Giotto, Fra Angelico, and Perugino, though later they turned to Raphael, Signorelli, and Michelangelo for inspiration. Their solution was to reinterpret in their own style the poetic and naive art of the Early Renaissance and the monumentality of the High Renaissance. While copying these earlier styles they spoke much of the importance of sentiment; but they saw only the surface of the masterpieces, not the depths. For this reason their production has a quaint religiosity, rather weak and hesitating. Determination alone cannot make an art movement, though the poet Goethe thought they had created one.

Many French artists whose styles differ grew to maturity in David's studio. David wanted each student to cultivate his particular talent, preferring a good small master to a bad great one. His own work indicated more than one direction to his disciples. In his famous *Coronation of Napoleon* of 1805-7 his colorful pageant turns under a great hovering web of embracing space; this and other paintings done for Napoleon set the stage for the grandiose pictorial machines that were to proclaim the hero to the world: scenes of battle, victory, and diplomatic maneuver followed one another in quick sequence. The most gifted of the new military painters was Antoine Jean Gros (1771-1835), whose scenes of Napoleon's battles at Eylau and Aboukir introduce new pre-Romantic concepts in painting: diagonals carry moving columns of men and horses into the stress of battle, weaving uneven patches of light and color over the charged surfaces of the canvas. Elsewhere, even when using a more studied way of building space, Gros brings innovations derived from Italian paintings that he once admired in Italy; in the *Pesthouse of Jaffa* of 1804 the fearless General Bonaparte touches the plague-stricken, who writhe about him within circles of gloomy shadow. Light and shadow break up the interior of this pesthouse to heighten the dramatic intensity of the story. Anne-Louis Girodet (1767-1824) also painted military scenes, but his are characterized by suave color and soft rendering of figures engaged in declamatory gesturing. Both he and Gros attempted to use free and spontaneous brushwork, the latter's often broken and approximate as he painted eagerly and quickly. François Gérard (1770-1837), the most successful among the Davidians, painted portraits of celebrities. Called the painter of princes and the prince of painters, he created a regal decor for the Napoleonic royalty; in his grand manner great draperies sweep majestically above a confident new aristocracy.

The portrait in Napoleonic France sometimes drew on British precedents, as painters traveled back and

1. Lawrence: *Julia, Lady Peel*. About 1825.
Copyright: the Frick Collection, New York.

2. Stuart: *Captain Henry Rice*. 1815.
Metropolitan Museum of Art, New York.

3. Bonington: *Parterre of Versailles*. 1826.
Louvre, Paris. (Arch. Photo)

Blake: *And the Morning Stars Sang
Together, from the Book of Job*. 1820.
Morgan Library Collection, New York.

forth across the channel, forced out by exile or lured by patronage. Madame Vigée-Lebrun was at home in either country. In fashionable eighteenth-century London Joshua Reynolds in his great-master style and Thomas Gainsborough in an opulent Van Dyck tradition prepared the way for others. Thomas Lawrence (1769-1830) continued the tradition of silk and satin spread artfully against a lavish background. His style supplied the essential note of grandeur and affected French portraitists. George Romney (1734-1802) painted in a broader style. Henry Raeburn (1756-1823), John Hoppner (1758-1810), and George Harlow (1787-1819) all contribute to the British tradition of portraiture.

With the increased circulation of the printed word and image more artists turned to various kinds of printmaking. In England John Flaxman (1755-1826) illustrated Homer's work with simple linear illustrations; in these most of the detail was sacrificed to an outline stressing his graceful figures. The French Primitives examined his work with interest and often imitated his subjects. William Blake (1757-1827) conceived of a more fluid line, which was not only to evoke the substance of the figures but also to endow them with a surging lyrical movement; an original mysticism and a desire for universal spiritual harmony animate his work. As a poet too Blake attempted to make more flexible the costume world the word drew on, inventing new characters as he invented new techniques for the printed image. His contribution was so personal and unusual that in his own time his message went almost unheard. Like other moralists Blake was interested in ideas first and built up a system of morality and action revealed in line. Those who utilize color and shadows and contrasting masses are more concerned with the visible world, with action and pleasure. The imaginative Swiss-English Henry Fuseli (1741-1825), attracted to literary sources for his themes, described a supernatural world of light and dark in which linear forms are caught as in a web.

In the early part of the nineteenth century the English water-colorists, breaking from the topographical manner of the Italianate tradition, began to rediscover nature in their own countryside. Using transparent and fluid colors applied in broad washes or minute scintillating detail, they described valleys and villages seen

Goya: *3 May 1808 in Madrid.*
Prado, Madrid. (Anderson-Giraudon)

under distant blue skies or against cloud-gathering hills, wayfarers and shepherds traversing winding country roads ("Nature . . . in her genuine simplicity," as Wordsworth said of such work), or the tangle of quotidian city streets shaded by leaning houses. Thomas Girtin (1775-1802), John Cotman (1782-1842), David Cox (1783-1859), and young William Turner (1775-1851) excel in evocations of the natural unfolding world, whose boundaries were enlarged by such pantheistic poets as Wordsworth and Coleridge hinting of mystery concealed in all natural phenomena.

In America the British and French portrait traditions were much in vogue, though many portraitists

Prud'hon: *Empress Josephine*. 1805.
Louvre, Paris. (Arch. Photo)

were itinerant salesmen, limners who filled in faces on prepainted opulent backgrounds. Some American artists, such as Gilbert Stuart (1775-1828), went to Europe to study. John Singleton Copley (1738-1815) stayed in England and there became eminent in the field of portraiture. Benjamin West (1738-1820) achieved greatness in history painting; his sublime and naive pastiches, artfully arranged and forceful in their rendering, were accorded great respect. He eventually became President of the Royal Academy in London. The Davidian John Vanderlyn (1775-1852) always stressed his Gallic allegiance. J. J. Audubon (1785-1851) went to France to study with David and in time decided to cultivate his own native idiom at home, where he became successful as an artist and ornithologist.

In Spain the Napoleonic era was a time of disaster for Francisco Goya (1746-1828), nourished in his country on Titian and Rubens, on seventeenth-century Spanish masters, and on the free Rococo styles of the eighteenth century. Living through the turmoil of a war-ravaged country, Goya reacted passionately: in his work the *Third of May 1808* the somber diagonals formed by the rifles of the implacable though unseen soldier-executioners are opposed to the disorder of the terror-stricken victims—all devoured by a terrible light that transfixes the scene. Goya uses his brush freely, patching together fragments of light and dark, his compositional arrangements appearing almost accidental and his figures unposed. Such unintellectual and emotional work is a personal expression of feeling leading to the Romantic world of violent passion on the one hand and to social protest on the other.

There is a smaller current remaining from the eighteenth century in European art: genre, a kind of art drawing upon subjects from everyday life, often the middle-class activity that had also been the subject of Dutch seventeenth-century artists. Louis Boilly (1761-1845) preferred scenes of daily life where young women in nacreous white satin and long flowing Empire robes pose gracefully with pretty children and gallant husbands. Eighteenth-century England produced the great Hogarth; in the next century David Wilkie (1785-1841) with his bustling contemporary scenes, drawing on coarse seventeenth-century Dutch and Flemish models, enjoyed wide popularity. Genre was an art of small dimension, and often its practitioners turned to a practical kind of portraiture: nothing ennobled and everything recorded. At that time portraiture, though generally conceded to be a secondary occupation for an artist, ranked among the more remunerative activities because almost everyone who could afford it wanted his likeness for posterity.

But in France the path to success lay in imitating the styles of David or the Davidians and in being accepted in the salon, the state-sponsored exhibition held about every two years in the Louvre. Pierre Paul Prud'hon (1758-1823) avoided the hard and sharp outlines of his Davidian friends; he preferred soft and diffuse shadows, *sfumato* similar to that used by Leonardo da Vinci, and mellow forms and agreeable colors echoing Correggio. His early romantic tendencies were unusual for his times, but because of his talent he won the admiration of his contemporaries and was even awarded government commissions. P. N. Guérin (1774-1833) adhered to the Davidian school;

1. Guérin: *Phaedra and Hippolytus.*
1802. Louvre, Paris. (Arch. Photo)

2. Géricault: *Raft of the "Medusa."*
1819. Louvre, Paris. (Arch. Photo)

a highly considered painter, he attracted to his studio young men of outstanding talent, two among whom were to shape the history of the unfolding century: Delacroix and Géricault.

Théodore Géricault (1791-1824) did not live long, but within the boundaries of his activity he brought to focus all that was best in European art to make of it a highly personal and dramatic vehicle for his own talent. In Italy he was impressed by Michelangelo and other Italian masters, in England by animal painters such as George Stubbs and in France by the men of the preceding generation: Prud'hon, David, Guérin, Girodet, and especially Gros. His important work is the *Raft of the Medusa,* inspired by the ordeal of ship-wrecked men and their rescue after forty anguished days on a raft. After two years' work Géricault exhibited his enormous painting in the Salon of 1819. Géricault's painting looked quite different from the others: his composition was turned off its horizontal axis—an axis most proper painters respected—so that a dramatic diagonal sweeps across the canvas from the father and dying son in the lower left to the Negro signaling the ship at the apex of the composition. The eye of the spectator is swept ruthlessly along, through audacious and vigorous brushwork. Greens and blacks are used freely to describe the tragedy: the suffering of the living, the putrefaction of the dead. In his passion

1

1. Houdon: *Sabine Houdon*.
1791. Louvre, Paris.
(Arch. Photo)

2. Chinard: *Portrait
of a Lady*. 1802.
Louvre, Paris. (Arch. Photo)

3. Clodion: *Bacchus
and Nymph with Cupid*.
Metropolitan Museum of Art,
New York. (Benjamin
Altman bequest)

Canova: *Pauline Bonaparte as Venus*. 1805-08.
Galleria Borghese, Rome. (Photo Alinari)

and turbulence Géricault turned a page in the history of painting.

His close friend Eugène Delacroix (1799-1863) continued in Géricault's steps. A highly literate man, he was inspired by the England he had visited and its authors he had read. Reaching out to Europe's cultural past and historical present, he formed the circle of his imagination with Dante and Goethe, with Byron and Scott. His varied literary subjects are conceived in a Rubenesque manner in which all the tranquil classical Poussinesque style is left behind and in its place bright colors in fluid shapes swirl into the excited Romantic world of painting; there the universe is alive with shifting masses and restless energy.

Sculpture in the second half of the eighteenth and the early nineteenth century echoed the activity in painting as it moved from the palpitating prettiness of intimate subjects to the ambitious monumentality of the early nineteenth-century imperial mania. In small complex Rococo sculpture Clodion's nymphs and fawns dally exotically on the wet terracotta landscape, their pliant surfaces revealing the sculptor's thumb nervously etching sensual volumes for the intimate appreciation of privileged connoisseurs. Pajou and others were similar in their Boucher-like concept of figures, preferring small-sized fragile works which seem destined for a boudoir. Monumental sculpture striving to be impressive could not escape this close personal accent, though by complicated allegories it attempted to be sublime and imposing. Shortly after the middle of

Schadow: *Two Princesses*.
1797. (Foto Marburg)

the eighteenth century, with the renewed appreciation of the ancient world, sculptors began to be influenced by classical works. The delightful scaled-down world of the Rococo sculptor gradually shed its superfluous details as it grew to impressive size with its message of antiquity, morality, and victorious didacticism. Contemporary celebrities made their appearance in heroic classical garb: the gifted J. A. Houdon (1741-1828) sculpted a full-sized classical Voltaire and a contem-

porary George Washington. His talent survived the weighty demands of monumentality, for despite their size his works are always alive with flickering light searching out the intimate contours of the surfaces. His portrait busts, his daughter Sabine or classical Benjamin Franklin, vibrate with the conviction of an immediate humanity. His contemporaries Joseph Chinard, F. J. Bosio, and A. D. Chaudet sometimes capture this same quality.

The Italian Antonio Canova (1757-1822) made no such compromise with the appeal of sensuous surface detail. Intent on the grandiose and the historically sublime, he copied directly from the ancients, though keeping one eye on the reality he was reproducing; his aim was not the portrait but the portrait-type, so that his patron Napoleon would be as easily recognized as Caesar or Alexander. In this he was supported by the archaeologist Quatremère de Quincy, who decided that Canova was neither a plagiarist despite his dependence on antiquity nor a forger of ancient sculpture. Balancing the ideal with the reality with which it must always be compared, a Neoclassical sculptor might arrive at that happy compromise where talent merges the two. Canova's heroes are often cold and mystifying, deprived of emotion and humanity, every pose contrived, exaggerated, and artificial. Nevertheless in some works Canova fulfills his mission, as in his *Venus*, where the lovely Pauline Bonaparte holding the apple of beauty reclines on a slablike couch emphasizing the body's front and back profiles. The marble surfaces are vibrant in their delicate simplicity; elegant detail there is too in profusion, but carefully related to the smooth expanse of the nude body enfolded in its precise décor.

Canova's sleek style greatly influenced his generation everywhere in Europe. The Dane Bertel Thorwaldsen (1768-1844) linearized and flattened it in bas-reliefs, though emphasizing the humanity of his scenes; such students and disciples as R. Westmacott (1775-1856) and John Gibson (1790-1866) brought Canova's style to England, where John Flaxman and Joseph Nollekens (1737-1823) worked in a confident insular idiom on their vast production of marble portraits. A competent Neoclassicism prevailed in Germany. Johann Heinrich von Dannecker (1758-1841) sculpted his *Ariadne on a Panther,* and David's friend Friedrich Tieck a *Priam at the Feet of Achilles.* Gottfried Schadow (1764-1850) tempered his antique with a frank realism in his royal commissions and used modern costumes for his heroes, as did Christian Rauch (1777-1857), though his tomb of Queen Louise of 1815 is classical and refined.

In architecture a classicism that had persisted in France from the time of Louis XIV began toward the end of the eighteenth century to be interpreted with a certain individual fantasy. In his bold engravings the Italian Piranesi (1720-78) had reconstructed a fantastic ancient Rome of fabulous monumentality, the buildings soaring and the interiors crushing any uneasy occupant by their very vastness; such scenes inspired architects in giving a grandiose note to their structures. In France Claude Nicolas Ledoux (1736-1806) ambitiously drew up the plans for the great salt factory at Chaux, complete in its details for administration buildings and housing for employees: great cubical structures, often quite unrelieved by exterior decoration, were arranged majestically (even at the

1. McComb: *Hamilton Grange.*
1802. New York.

2. Ledoux: *House for the Surveyor of the Loue.* 1804.

3. Soufflot: *Panthéon.* Paris.
1757-90. (Arch. Photo)

1

expense of windows) in a circle. In his house for the surveyor of the Loue River he conceived of a cylinder on its side: the upper part was given to habitation; through the lower part a river flowed. Cubes, circles, parallel rectangular constructions were the moving spirit of Ledoux's plans, such as his custom houses built at the gates of Paris. C. L. Clérisseau felt that there was no limit to this expanding architecture, which he later transported to Russia. E. L. Boullée and J. J. Lequeu designed in a similar monumental geometric style, as did J. L. Desprez in Sweden.

There were more restrained interpretations of the classical spirit based on the monuments of ancient Rome itself. Soufflot in France had in 1757 designed

a building reaching back to the grandeur of Rome by way of the High Renaissance: his Panthéon in Paris. Peyre stressed enormity in construction and clear opposition of open and closed façade space. Jean Chalgrin (1739-1811) in his Paris church of Saint-Philippe-du-Roule worked with unbroken heavy monumental walls relieved by the severest of porticoes.

By the end of the eighteenth century, architecture, like the other arts, had been affected by the new archaeological approach to antiquity and the search for the true spirit of Greece and Rome. A style in architecture, furniture, and decorative arts called Louis XVI in France and Adam in England prevailed, ·a style using motifs of an ancient civilization to enhance its own sober and elegant constructions. In general two styles were derived from the ancients: one employed on the exteriors, was heavy; the other, using Pompeian motifs and Greek ornament, was light and gracious and found its greatest application in the interiors. The sixteenth-century Italian Palladio often persisted in the ground plans. With the antique ornament applied to its flat surfaces, Neoclassical architecture was characterized by simplicity of space and perfection of line, by severity of contour, by good taste and lack of exaggeration.

During the Napoleonic era Neoclassical architecture, prevailing not only in France but all over the Western world, pretended to be a reversion to classical principles, though in practice it reinterpreted them. In France the leading architects were the team of Charles Percier (1764-1838) and Pierre Fontaine (1762-1853). In imperial palaces and residences their constructions are lightened with an eighteenth-century charm, the decoration flattened discreetly over the sober surfaces. On an essentially cubic construction forms are cut sharply from imposing rectangular masses, relieved by columns to enhance and vary the monumentality of heavy walls. The Church of the Madeleine, begun in 1808 by Pierre Vignon (1763-1828), and the 1808 Stock Exchange of Alexandre Brongniart (1739-1813) are excellent examples of this classic massiveness; they stress a Parisian consanguinity with Imperial Rome, so boastfully displayed in Percier and Fontaine's Arch of Triumph of the Carrousel and the famous Arch of Triumph at the Etoile (begun in 1806 by Chalgrin). The completion of many Napoleonic monuments took decades, and in their prolonged construction they influenced architecture for a long time.

The Empire style, exportable to all parts of the world where its spirit was welcomed, was given a chance to develop in another empire, that of the Tsars. Catherine the Great had already employed Clérisseau; and under Alexander I (who reigned from 1801 to 1825) the French imperial style was known as the Alexandrine style. Alexander carefully studied every drawing of Percier and Fontaine and employed Neoclassical French architects to make Petersburg one of the most fascinating of cities, with expansive vistas on a grandiose scale. Thomas de Thomon (1754-1831) in his Stock Exchange employed heavy columns in a peripteral temple; Ledoux elements appear in the Mine School of Voronkhine and Zakharov, while in the Admiralty Building the latter imitated his teacher Chalgrin. The reconstruction of Moscow after the fire of 1812 gave scope to such Neoclassical Italianate archi-

tects as Karl Ivanovich Rossi (1775-1849).

Germany saw the new style in a more scholarly way, preferring the austere purity of the Greek. In Berlin K. G. Langhans used a severe Doric grandeur in his Brandenburg Gate of 1790; and a painstaking seriousness appeared with Karl von Schinkel (1781-1841) in his theater with its classical porch and pediments and his museum with a peristyle colonnade. In Munich Louis I employed Leo von Klenze (1784-1864) to build a group of buildings in emulation of ancient Athens: in 1816 a neo-Greek Glyptothek to shelter the famous sculptures from the Greek temple at Aegina, and in 1846-63 two sturdy pylons flanking a propylaeum

2

3

reminiscent of that on the Athenian Acropolis. In a Pinakothek and other works of art a naive erudition characterizes this attempt to emulate and imitate antique models. Tsar Nicholas I employed Klenze on the Hermitage in Petersburg.

In England the Neoclassic style had been in vogue in the latter part of the eighteenth century, with the elegant and fine achievement of the Adams brothers. The Regency of George IV, bent on outdoing Napoleon, favored the monumental in units and in groups, like the complex Regent's Street and Park by John Nash (1752-1835). His Carlton House Terrace rises from a bold row of cast-iron columns; Chester Terrace presents balconies alternating with columned façades. Cumberland Terrace, done in collaboration with James Thomson, remains a monument of Neoclassical planning where successive elements are unified in an extended project. Nash's Brighton Pavilion is a fantastic excursion into the oriental and the picturesque. Archaeologist, traveler, collector, John Soane (1753-1837) in his own house at Lincoln's Inn Fields employed sparse incised mouldings for its decoration, while urns and statuary emphasize the lean vertical movement of the exterior, as they do in his own house in Ealing with its affixed triumphal arch and rounded forms alternating with large rectangular ones. Dublin's post office of 1815 by Francis Johnston (1760-1829), with its plain and well-composed façade with Ionic porch, and Glasgow's Royal Exchange of 1829 by David Hamilton, its eight Corinthian columns surmounted by a severe pediment and a monument to Lysicrates, are fine examples of this period. The cast-iron bridges of John Rennie (1761-1821) and the simple docks and warehouses of

Thomas Telford (1757-1834) made their important contribution to architecture.

In the United States several styles had been inherited from Europe: in the North the English tradition of Adam carried on with Charles Bulfinch (1763-1844), Samuel McIntire (1757-1811), and John McComb, whose New York City Grange of 1802 for Alexander Hamilton remains one of the fine examples of Anglo-French neoclassicist tendencies absorbed into a native American idiom; the severe elegance of its proportions and the simplicity of the exterior and interior design keep the construction well within a long tradition, extending from colonial to modern Park Avenue archi-

Thomon: *Marine Stock Exchange*. 1804-16. Petersburg.

1

2

48

1. Soane: *House at Lincoln's Inn Fields*.
1813. London. (Photo Herbert-Felton)

2. Schinkel: *Theater*. 1819-21. Berlin.
(Archiv für Kunst und Geschichte, Berlin)

3. Nash: *Carlton House Terrace*. London.
1828-42. (British Information Service)

4. Klenze: *Glyptothek*. 1816-30. Munich.

1. Jefferson: *University of Virginia.*
1817-26. Charlottesville, Va.

2. Latrobe, Hallet, Thornton, Bulfinch:
U. S. Capitol. 1792-1828. Washington, D. C.

1

2

tecture, of flat surfaces supported by lean skeletons. In the South the French tradition prevailed. Jefferson, an ardent archaeologist-architect impressed by the Maison Carrée at Nîmes and other Roman buildings, was dedicated to Neoclassicism; a Franco-Roman republican style animates his design for the University of Virginia with its porticoed galleries and Roman Pantheon. For the city of Washington Pierre L'Enfant planned radiating boulevards as spokes cutting across a gridiron plan. Jefferson's friend Benjamin Latrobe (1764-1820), after initial work by E. S. Hallet and W. Thornton, raised the Capitol's great Pantheon-like central portion with pediment and covering dome; after 1817 Bulfinch continued the work.

In an age of increased manufacture and industrial revolution European monarchs and their entourages encouraged luxury industries in pottery, porcelain, jewelry, silks, and stuffs because their production was synonymous with prosperity. In an ever-growing market a tradition of excellent craftsmanship flourished for the old and new clientele. Still admired today are the fine pieces of furniture by Jacob and bronzes by Odiot, Biennais, and Thomire in France; furniture by Sheraton and silver by Storr in England. Against a background of rectangular elegance in interior decoration the furniture grew sturdier, its severe polished lines and classical ornamentation heavier; strong lion's legs, caryatids, and sphinxes in bright bronze supported simple tables and chairs enlivened with laurel and meander motifs. An angular style became popular all over Europe; other countries accepted it because, done by skilled craftsmen, it was always in good taste. In the next generation machine-made products competed more

and more with the work of the skilled artisan.

New museums, open to the public, were enriched with works from all parts of the world. The Napoleonic era sent art works all over Europe. Ancient sculptures, Italian and Spanish paintings made their way to France. With the downfall of Napoleon in 1815 and the dispersion of many masterpieces to their former owners, or to new owners—and the appearance of dealers eager to facilitate the passage of art from collection to collection—the great European public became more aware of the accessibility of art. In England and Germany the acquisition of the famous Elgin and Aegina marbles, and in France of the Venus de Milo, spurred competition among collectors, while the public awareness of archaeology deepened.

Setting the stage for the future, the first quarter of the nineteenth century witnessed an increase in the number of art patrons from the bourgeoisie, who com-

1. Goya: *Misfortune in the Stands*. 1815. Etching and aquatint.

2. Thomire: *Candelabra*. 1815-25. Metropolitan Museum of Art, New York.

missioned portraits and bought works of the artist after his successful exhibitions. An unsuccessful artist experienced acute distress in an overcrowded field. The print, a medium undergoing new development, was a less expensive art product available to a wider public. The new technique of lithography attracted such men as Géricault, whose dramatic plates combine the best of English and French traditions. Goya produced a memorable series of etchings. And the art critics multiplied, current interpreters of the art work for the new public.

The new patrons, an undefined public, unsure of their own taste and often conscious of the lack of it, plunged into the problem of aesthetics and clamored for their share of the beautiful, yearning for the opulence and status of ownership. The aristocracy still flourished, but shared the symbols of its class with those who could afford such identification.

2
ROMANTICISM

1825-1850

Ingres: *Odalisque with Slave*. 1842.
Walters Art Gallery, Baltimore.

■ In the important Salon of 1824 Eugène Delacroix exhibited his *Massacre of Chios,* a painting dealing with the murder of Greeks during their recent rebellion. Passion and pain play a conspicuous part in this work: death and bodily corruption move through the vanquished and despairing figures; terror and anguish are boldly evident; while the pathetic, from helpless children to doomed old people, strike a compassionate note as the artist takes his stand on a contemporary issue. His contrasting macabre colors partake of the despairing mood that we found in Géricault's *Raft of the Medusa.* At this same salon Ingres, after eighteen years of self-exile in Italy, also appeared with the *Vow of Louis XIII,* a large painting showing the French king kneeling before the Madonna and Child and asking Her protection for France. Calm contours and clear colors are harmoniously arranged in a balanced composition. The theme, style, and technique are derived from Raphael; Ingres admitted this, though at the same time maintaining that he was a French painter.

The year 1824 prepared the great struggle of Romantic and Classic art, Delacroix championing the former and Ingres, with the Davidians, the latter. The contest of these two schools echoes the rivalry of Rubenist and Poussinist painting in the seventeenth century. The Davidians attempted to remain within a humanist Poussinist tradition appealing to the intellect, a tradition derived from the ancients: clarity and simplicity, the good, ideal, and beautiful. Ingres felt that it was the artist's task to find an immutable world of perfection, of ideals never varying from century to century and valid to ancients and moderns alike. To create forms in which so fine a balance prevails that nothing could touch it, nor any personal emotion intrude on it, he isolated each figure within a strong linear boundary keeping it within its own undisturbed sphere, almost like a perfect diagram. Line becoming the most important element of expression, color was simply used as a map to set apart and harmonize one form with another, while everything remained complete and clear, nothing unfinished and no errant brush strokes visible. Shadows were reduced to keep the planes flat, equalized, and harmonious throughout, and to tone down the abrupt transition from light to dark. Later, after Impressionism had dissolved the finely contained world, painters returned to this concept: this was the case with Degas, Cézanne, Renoir, and Gauguin. After World War I, Picasso imitated Ingres, and Matisse and Gorky had much praise for him.

For the Romantics, art could not be limited to the ideal good and beautiful, for nature and human beings are not one-sided but many-sided, intuitive and irrational, sensual and imperfect. The artist's passion transforms and unifies the material into a work of art. In Romantic painting human emotions are stressed; out of the disquietude of the painter the vision of the world is conceived, a vision personal and forceful. Pain and sorrow and extremes of every emotion enter and are echoed by the uneasy universe containing them. Sickness, blood, death, terror, and violence are often

Delacroix: *Massacre at Chios.*
1824. Louvre, Paris. (Arch. Photo)

Ingres: *Vow of Louis XIII*. 1824.
Cathedral of Montauban, France. (Arch. Photo)

encountered, for the Romantic artist and poet were embroiled in an uneasy and seething society in the throes of change. The Romantics championed a vivid Rubenesque approach to painting, deforming and interpreting nature to emphasize the drama they found there : not immutable ideal forms, but forms in motion, masses modeled with sweeping strokes of color that appealed to the senses. Inspired and imaginative, they advocated fantastic, exotic, mysterious, distant, and unusual scenes, more literary than real. In 1827 Victor Hugo in his preface to *Cromwell* advocated the juxtaposition of conflicting elements in a work of art : the ugly and beautiful, the dark and light, the serious and comic; in this way he clarified the Romantic stand. In that year Delacroix's *Death of Sardanapalus* exhibited a reposeful and undismayed monarch contemplating the fire, fury, and murder in his burning palace. The violence of the scene is matched by an unbridled brush which mixes warm and rich blues, reds, and greens in the opulent manner of seventeeth-century Peter-Paul Rubens. That same year Devéria showed an ugly dwarf setting off fine courtiers (following Hugo's suggestion) and Delacroix painted *Tasso in the Madhouse*. The Romantics went back into the history of France or to their favorite poets and dramatic writers: Byron, Vigny, Hugo, Goethe, Shakespeare; or, like Delacroix and Decamps, were inspired with the exotic Near East. Hugo himself in his water colors and washes excelled in supernatural fantasy,

Constable: *The Hay Wain*. 1821.
National Gallery. London.

where twilight and night are vehement in their passage
through mountains and the ruins of cities.

The Salon of 1824 was conspicuous for the impressive English participation by such men as Bonington
and Constable. Richard Bonington (1801-28), a friend
of Delacroix, mediated between France and England.
He is best known for his landscapes of great breadth
bathed in the luminosity of blue skies and green fields,
the vastness of sweep of vision his British contemporaries admired. In freshness and clarity of presentation
he was matched by John Constable (1776-1837), intent
on the fleeting, the intangible and changeable aspects
of nature with its capricious daily moods. Constable's

Turner: *The Slave Ship*. 1837.
Museum of Fine Arts, Boston.

oil sketches are industrious jottings-down of how his
model Nature appeared in all her subtle transforma-
tions, from field and clouds to stream and village; to
the site he adds mood and temperament, atmosphere
and enveloping season. The optimism in Constable gave
way to something more luridly Romantic in the later
Turner: the site disintegrates under the heavy atmospheric effects and the transient seasons; for the shifting
phenomena of the scene are more important than the
scene itself dissolving in light and absorbed by the
accidents of weather. Turner observed such things in
the paintings of Claude Lorrain (1600-82), where light
disintegrates all solidity and the hardness of the world

turns into the softness of the artist's vision. Forms are no longer identifiable in Turner's last works; steam, smoke, fog, daybreak, and twilight become the subjects of the landscapes. The extremes in his painting technique are matched by those in his wild literary evocations of disaster and terror on land and at sea.

The French landscape tradition was quite different; what was accidental and illogical in nature must be made to fit an orderly pattern; and the twists of the valley roads that the English admired for their picturesqueness were in France used to clarify the movement from one plane of the landscape to the next, so that all became as carefully arranged as a formal French garden. This was the classical and orderly way; and in French landscape painting a long tradition connects David's Luxembourg and Ingres' Medici Gardens with Valenciennes' and Corot's scenes; or the landscapes in Poussin and Claude with those in the work of Cézanne and the Cubist painters. Clarity of the most perplexing order, relevance and contiguity in the most contrived manner, integrity of space, and explicit means are all part of the French tradition; and insofar as such other nations as Italy and Russia embraced her tradition, it characterized their art too.

Camille Corot (1796-1875) shows in his early work the striving of a passionate pilgrim to record the great sites in Italy and France; here are a series of clear flat planes in broad patches of landscape muted in soft colors, and of sunlit volumes of buildings arranged placidly over the picture space. In later interior scenes he poses melancholy women molded by Italianate chiaroscuro and engrossed in private dreams.

In 1825 David died and his doctrine was carried on

by his disciples and imitators, by Ingres and by the new head of the school, Baron Gros. The Ingres disciples, such as Hippolyte Flandrin in his Paris church murals, cultivated the noble and serene in their work, drawing heavily on the Italian quattrocento and shunning Davidian sculptural mass for Ingrist linearism. Many of Ingres' students are remembered for their part in teaching the generation of Impressionist and later schools, and many for their individual contributions. Théodore Chassériau (1819-56) in his *Two Sisters* reveals the influence of Ingres in the conception of the figure and its construction, though he adds a color and mood that are derived from Delacroix.

It was difficult to continue in the old Neoclassical tradition; Gros himself suffered from his inability to make it palatable. It was easier to carry on David's other tradition: grandiose portrayals of contemporary Napoleonic scenes where with melodramatic fervor figures declaimed the history of their time. In 1815 when the Emperor was exiled, the restored Bourbon king of France was willing to patronize artists who painted these great historical canvases, ordered for such royal palaces as Versailles and Saint-Cloud and for the churches and public buildings where ambitious and edifying scenes recalled the Bourbon and national glory.

The second quarter of the century is the domain of those recognized masters who were awarded important government commissions in palaces and churches. This encouragement of monumental art fostered the grandiose. While the Romanticists and Classicists searched ancient and French dynastic history and European fiction for their themes, another school was forming,

1. Corot: *Cathedral of Chartres.* 1830.
Louvre, Paris. (Arch. Photo)

2. Chasseriau: *Two Sisters.*
1843. Louvre, Paris. (Arch. Photo)

headed by such men as Paul Delaroche (1797-1856)
and Horace Vernet (1789-1863). This school was the
result of erudition artists acquired as part of their
training, especially in the Paris Ecole des Beaux-Arts
(School of Fine Arts). These men strove to be correct
and to avoid the two extremes of painting: the Classical, which improved its subjects by making them ideal
and perfect; and the Romantic, which distorted them
to emphasize their dramatic qualities. In this third
school, called the *Juste Milieu* (Just or Golden Means,
the Happy Medium), classical models and antique para-
phernalia in the decor were arranged with attenuated
Romantic emotions and literary contrivances. Moving
through the bric-à-brac of his theatrical world, the successful painter transcribed everything in its literal and
prosaic context. There a chair is a chair, neither the
Platonic immutable chair of the Classicists nor the
agonized chair reflecting man's anxiety, as in the work
of Delacroix (whom Van Gogh copied). Though not
interested in the *trompe-l'oeil* (fool-the-eye) technique
of illusion, they presented a world as clear and as
readily identifiable as the objects in the newly invented
photograph—their formidable rival. Through the nineteenth century this *Juste Milieu* tradition, gathering
elements of either school and fitting them into a for-
mula, was championed by successful painters against
whom the Impressionists later struggled.

1. Vernet: *Mazeppa.* 1826.
Calvet Museum, Avignon.

2. Delaroche: *The Children
of Edward IV in the Tower of London.*
1830. Louvre, Paris. (Giraudon)

1

2

At the same time a new realism appeared with Victor Hugo and other writers and painters. Baron Gros in the beginning of the century had painted realistic battle scenes, adapted none the less to the taste of the Napoleonic censors; his admirer Géricault continued this tradition of depicting the dead or the agonies of the dying, as did Delacroix in the *Massacre of Chios;* by 1835 with Boissard de Boisdenier's *Episode of the Retreat from Moscow* the realism of this tradition is established. In this realistic trend is also the Romantic interest in distressing and disquieting subjects.

In Germany the cult of the supernatural prevailed in such scenes as *Macbeth and the Witches* of Joseph Anton Koch (1768-1839), where circular waves and windswept trees caught in a compelling rhythm melodramatically unify the composition; or in his romantic landscapes with distant mountains bathed in snow and clouds. Early in the century Caspar David Friedrich (1774-1840) imagined such overpowering, awe-inspiring scenes, later to become characteristic of his work as *Abbey Graveyard Under Snow;* here shorn winter trees crackling with snow frame a procession of monks onto a ruined stage set of a twilit Gothic cathedral. A mysterious space leads into the background. Effects of moonlight, mist, and twilight abound in his original and mystic works.

In the United States at this time the Turneresque Thomas Cole (1801-48) painted huge historical visions of the rise and fall of empires, and Asher B. Durand (1796-1886) romantic landscapes filled with keen observation for picturesque natural details. Others such as William S. Mount (1807-68) and George C. Bingham (1811-79) painted genre scenes of the life around

them, the latter's *Fur Traders Descending the Missouri*
is a fine example of a local subject described in terms
of an economical and even amusing composition and
unusual atmospheric effects.

In Russia the gifted Karl Brullow (1799-1852) attracted much attention with the *Last Day of Pompei*,
about 1830, done in a post-Davidian idiom; his Romanticism is apparent in *Countess Samilov and Her
Daughter*, a lively and interestingly arranged work.
Determined to produce a Russian non-Western work,
Alexandre Ivanov (1806-58) painted during two decades his *Apparition of Christ to the People*, a mixture
of Renaissance and Poussinesque painting seen through
Nazarene eyes; idealism struggles with realism in this
huge canvas, which has some fine passages though the
over-all effect is heavy.

The sculpture of this generation shows its alliances
with painting. Disciples of Canova and Thorwaldsen
spread the Neoclassical styles ever thinner and weaker.
Critic Gautier doubted that there could ever be a
Romantic style because "sculpture seems to have received from antiquity its definitive form." Lorenzo
Bartolini, Ingres' friend, made more palpitating and
energetic the suave forms in which antique tradition
merged with the Italian; and his compatriot Tenerani
returned to similar sources. James Pradier (1792-
1852) in France insisted on the classical norm; his

1. Bingham: *Fur Traders Descending the Missouri*.
1845. Metropolitan Museum of Art, New York.

2. Friedrich: *Abbey Graveyard Under Snow*. 1819.
(Archiv für Kunst und Geschichte, Berlin)

69

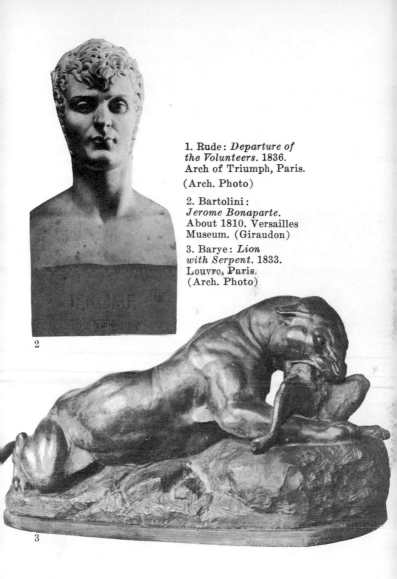

1. Rude: *Departure of the Volunteers*. 1836. Arch of Triumph, Paris. (Arch. Photo)

2. Bartolini: *Jerome Bonaparte*. About 1810. Versailles Museum. (Giraudon)

3. Barye: *Lion with Serpent*. 1833. Louvre, Paris. (Arch. Photo)

2

3

Psyche and *Atalante* have an affected antique seriousness at odds, as Baudelaire remarks, with their "coif-
fures of kept women." Elsewhere in Europe a Neoclassicism tempered by a refined realism prevailed in
sculpture destined for royal courts, as in the works of
the Germans Rauch and Schadow. In England Francis
Chantry (1781-1841) was the reputable sculptor of
such great men as Washington, Wellington, Scott, and
George IV, and his disciple Peter Hollins shows his
competence in the statue of Mrs. Thompson of 1838;
Samuel Joseph in his monument to William Wilber-
force of 1838 in Westminster Abbey reveals a talent
for striking and strong characterization.

A friend of the Romantics, many of whose portraits
he executed in bronze medallions, David d'Angers
(1788-1856) took great interest in their subtle physiog-
nomies as evocations of genius; he was able to group
great men in his pediment for the Paris Panthéon. The
gifted François Rude (1784-1855), awarded the commission for the *Departure of the Volunteers* on the
Paris Arch of Triumph, demonstrates his ability to in-
fuse forms with a new animation, the figures of the
group embraced into a unity by the maternal and war-
like presence of La Marseillaise.

Antoine Barye (1795-1875) sculpted animals that
have sloughed off the neoclassical veneer. A student
of Gros, he preferred violent themes of jungle beasts
and their prey; in *Lion and Serpent* of 1833 the exciting tension of devouring animal has its counterpart
in rhythmic muscle surfaces undulating in organic
convulsions. The writhing forms of hunter and victim
swirl in and out of light in the pulsating mass of his
bronzes, riddled with dark menacing voids, catching

the light dramatically on haunch or open jaw. Another great master of sculpture is Honoré Daumier with a rogue's gallery of eminent people, in which caricature turns into expressionism describing angularities of features or paunchiness of spirit.

In this period architects completed the Paris work begun during the Napoleonic era: the Church of the Madeleine and the Arch of Triumph, while Fontaine carried on the Neoclassical style in his interior decorations for the Louvre. An early Christian basilica plan with antique coffered ceiling appears in Le Bas' Notre-Dame-de-Lorette of 1823-36 with its graceful portico. Jacques Hittorff (1792-1867) planted terraces rising slowly to his two-towered Saint-Vincent-de-Paul in Paris, where polychrome plays an important part. Visitors to that city remember his ship-prowed lamp-posts on the Place de la Concorde and the string of small houses encircling the Arch of Triumph. A Renaissance revival appeared in such buildings as Lacornée's Foreign Ministry of 1846, with its thick relief of superimposed arches covering the noble façade fronting the Seine River on the Quai d'Orsay. Duban's restorations for the old Louvre in 1848 carried on a French Renaissance revival and set the style for many apartment buildings that give the city its lavish bourgeois aspect.

Outstanding for the 40's is the Library of Sainte-Geneviève of Henri Labrouste (1801-75); ironwork within spells out the large and light reading rooms, while its façade of elegant masonry parallels the Panthéon's great walled arms. Lenoir's Gare Montparnasse and other railroad stations use train sheds of glass webbed in iron arches, behind a severe and soberly proportioned stone façade. The Gothic style was re-

vived with Gau's Sainte-Clotilde in 1839 and the two
royal chapels in Dreux in 1839 and in Paris in 1844,
with Ingres as the leading decorator. Interest in the
Gothic grew with the restorations of the great cathe-
drals, medieval towns, and châteaux by Viollet-le-Duc.
In Germany Ahlert's Cologne Cathedral shows an
erudite interest in the country's Gothic past. Friedrich
von Gartner in the Munich National Library and Gottfried Semper in his Dresden Opera of 1837 stressed a
Renaissance tradition.

Elsewhere in Europe the Neoclassic tradition continued in church structures echoing the Roman and
Parisian Pantheons: Pietro Bianchi's San Francesco

di Paolo in Naples with its great Berniniesque colonnade; or in Russian Petersburg, Auguste Monferran's Saint Isaac's Cathedral (1817-57) with its great iron dome outsizing its Paris prototype, as does the same architect's monumental Alexander Column of 1829. Robert Smirke (1781-1867) planned the British Museum (1824-47), an Ionic Parthenon with sculptured pediment, flanked by two severe Ionic wings; a small piazza sets off its picturesque monumentality. Its profusion of columns is typical of the Greek and Roman penchant of the builders of this era. In the hands of the gifted Charles Barry (1795-1860) a Renaissance style was widely employed in mansions and clubhouses.

Smirke: *British Museum*, London.
1824-47. (British Information Service)

Strickland: *Merchants' Exchange,*
1832-4. Philadelphia.

Barry drew up plans for the Houses of Parliament in
1836, a building regular in plan with early Victorian
Gothic detail supplied by Augustus Pugin (1812-52),
who in church building insisted on the functional need
of the ritual.

In the United States the Neoclassical was the thriving style in domestic and public architecture. Fine
examples are found throughout the South and the
eastern seaboard in the grandiose mansions of planta-
tion owners or wealthy industrialists; or in such striking buildings as Philadelphia's Merchants' Exchange
of 1832 by William Strickland: a severe flat-walled
rectangular building modulates into thin pilasters and
a semicircular colonnade surmounted by a monument

Labrouste: *Library of Sainte-Geneviève.*
1843-50. (Arch. Photo)

of Lysicrates, the severe rectangular units of the ground floor acting as a contrasting stylobate. Traditional elements used in an original way to maintain fine proportions characterize Isaiah Rogers' Boston Tremont House of 1828, with its chaste flat façade and Doric porch, and his elaborate columniated Merchants Exchange of 1838. The Gothic, a style suitable for commercial and institutional architecture, also flourished in the young republic. Willard's Bowdoin Street Church of 1830 in Boston and Upjohn's Trinity Church of 1839-46 in New York are good examples. However, in the United States as elsewhere, most of the historical architectural styles were imitated and freely interpreted, sometimes with original innovations.

3

REALISM

1850–1875

Manet: *Luncheon on the Grass*. 1863.
Louvre, Paris. (Giraudon)

■ In the mid-century a new talent appears: Gustave Courbet (1819-77), shaped by social revolutionary ideas of 1848.

After a decade of participation in the official salons he opened a one-man exhibition in 1855 to protest against official painting. There he showed the *Burial at Ornans,* a long monotonous procession of ordinary village people whom the painter knew, their sober and rude faces absorbed in the business at hand. Black and solemnly-clad figures reveal a morose affinity with the clods of earth over which they move and with the death that mystically integrates them with the fresh-spaded ground. The dull colors heavily laid on seem allied to earth and peasant life. The whole atmosphere is reportorial, the figures unposed and caught in their quotidian essence. The scene evokes a personal and immediate memory in which neither classical idealization and timelessness nor Romantic fervor have any part.

At the great official exhibition of 1855 several painters were honored by special rooms within the art section; Ingres represented a sort of Classicism, Delacroix a thriving Romanticism, and Delaroche and Horace Vernet the persistent *Juste Milieu.* There were other famous painters with a personal style, though essentially they belonged to one of these groups. Courbet was his own school and in his private exhibi-

tion elsewhere defined his intention and gave it the
name of Realism. The challenge he offered was direct:
there should be no Art at all, artists should simply
portray the facts of life "as they are," without idealization, morality, or sentiment. "There are no schools,"
he said, "there are only painters," implying that art
could not be taught.

It may be imagined how his work struck the public
and his artist contemporaries who were struggling to
maintain in art an ideal world, whether Romantic or
Classical, and who still felt themselves to belong to
older artistic traditions. Courbet touched on Social
Realism, as in his *Stone Cutters*. He luxuriated in a
tactile greenness in his landscapes, his palette heavy
with floriating and vegetal nature, often thickly rendered with palette knife rather than brush. In other

Courbet, *Burial at Ornans.*
1849. Louvre, Paris.
(Arch. Photo)

works his proletarian sisters of Rubens' fleshy nudes
have no identity with the verdant scene but stand
solidly rooted like tree trunks to a ground resounding
to their heavy presence. His self-portraits and scenes
of lovers echo the indulgent Romanticism of his time.
He consciously alienated himself from the political
world of favors and recompense, emphasizing the artist
as an independent and isolated crusader, a world apart
from the society in which he uncomfortably found
himself.

The contemporary scene interested another artist:
Honoré Daumier (1808-79). His lithographs are important documents concerning the life of his time,
sympathetically describing the everyday existence of
Parisians he moved among, mocking the foibles of the
bourgeoisie and acidly criticizing the politicians who

1

1. Daumier: *Massacre on the Rue Transnonain.*
1834. Lithograph.

2. Courbet: *The Painter's Studio.*
1855. Louvre, Paris. (Giraudon)

2

Daumier: *Crispin and Scapin*.
1858-60. Louvre. (Arch. Photo)

mishandled the affairs of state. His lively and vehement
diatribes against the abuse of power and his scathing
attacks on the government continued over a period of
fifty years. Always occupied with his themes of injustice,
social inequity, and domestic irony, Daumier worked
in penury with but little time for the paintings and
drawings that have also given him a place in the history
of art. His message is carried by an excited linearity
writhing dramatically over the surface of his emo-
tionally surcharged work, bold and daring black lines
pulsing against white paper. His lithograph technique
is carried over into his drawings and paintings, where
simplified masses of darkness contrast daringly with

diffuse light. He worked in private on oils and drawings, never exhibiting them and rarely showing them to close friends. Daumier towers among numerous talented illustrators with whom he often collaborated in illustrated magazines and books: Gavarni, amusing and penetrating in tireless descriptions of the people he moved amongst, and Tony and Alfred Johannot.

Napoleon III's reign (1852-70), like Louis XVI's, was marked by an appreciation of nature; but if in the eighteenth century nature had been conceived through inspiration, free of the terrestrial restraints of daily living, in the later nineteenth century landscape became ordinary, proportionate to the spectator, and easily identifiable. Urban dwellers yearned for nature's simplicity and reverie-invoking moods, which the city stifled.

In his later years Corot developed a popular style of landscape dissolved in a soft monotony of silvery greens and grays often contrasted with sudden patches of red, the garment of a figure moving mysteriously through his volatile world. In the vaporous afternoon or twilight hour of enchantment evoking the forest's classical lore, studied nymphs and satyrs make their casual appearance. To these dreamlike scenes he gave such nostalgic titles as *Reverie* and *Memory*.

Corot was friendly with a younger group of painters who delighted in the Romantic and capricious appearances of nature and in its more ordinary aspects as well: the Barbizon school. Charles Daubigny (1817-78) and Théodore Rousseau (1812-67) painted scenes of the great forest of Fontainebleau near the village of Barbizon; they leaned heavily on seventeeth-century Dutch predecessors, stressing bulky trees against windswept backgrounds; but they also painted a humanized nature in tune with man and reflecting the emotions and reactions of human beings. Rousseau felt: "It is good composition when the objects represented are not there solely as they are, but when they contain under a natural appearance the sentiments which they have stirred in our souls." Jean Francois Millet (1814-75) was of this group; religious inspiration and sympathy with the humble toilers of the fields give his work a compassionate rustic mood, the rough daily life tempered by a soft vision where forms are rounded, almost weathered by man's alliances with the seasons.

It must be remembered that Ingres and Delacroix were still painting into the sixties; the Barbizons also painted into the sixties and seventies, when they finally became popular. Young innovators increasingly challenged the apathy and indifference of the bourgeoisie, their chief patrons. Courbet in his painting *The Studio* depicted the allegory of the artist's struggle with his Philistine public, preparing the ground for the next generation of artists whose dilemma in an inhospitable world was similar to his; while artists of other schools, stranded on the island of incommunicability, proclaimed art for art's sake and found in his espousal of life as opposed to art the precedent of their withdrawal from life. Courbet had already posed the problem whose solution artists were to seek in the rapidly succeeding *isms* with which they labeled their art: what areas of human experience belong to art, and how shall art portray them: what subject matter suits which style?

Ingres felt that the painting need not reflect the world of man at all, but rather its own world, the canvas becoming a universe in itself whose innate order, integrity, and perfection had little in common with the imperfect reality in which the spectator is kept at a distance. He felt the subject did not matter at all, and to inquiring young Degas he counseled: "Draw lines, lots of lines—from objects or from memory." For his linearism and his naive and flattened figures he was criticized as an "abstract painter." This pure and suigeneric world of forms was seized on by an Art-for-Art's-Sake movement and the aestheticism of the late nineteenth century in England and France, which conceived art not as mere representation but as a sacred world of beauty cultivated for its sake alone. Gautier championed Ingres while Baudelaire, fervent apostle of beauty for its own sake, exalted Delacroix; they and such other writers as Gustave Flaubert and Edmond and Jules de Goncourt created special worlds of refinement and sensibility into which they might retreat. Walter Pater and Oscar Wilde also retreated there.

In addition, the young generation was strongly attracted to that strand of Romanticism which explored the instinctive and irrational pockets of the mind, a strand found rewoven into Rimbaud's new system of poetry, in Gérard de Nerval, Nodier, and Lautréamont describing terrains merging into the unusual of the imagination; while in hallucinating drawings and engravings Grandville, Rodolphe Bresdin, and Félicien Rops—even Victor Hugo—were no less daring in their descent into the subconscious darkness. This Romantic current gives a literary flavor to the art movements echoing it and runs through Symbolism and Expressionism and finally the Surrealism of the 1930's.

These new tendencies, inward explorations, ignored

the surrounding world; however, there were also artists who continued to explore the exterior world, drawing on the Romanticist's vivid and immediate interest in man and nature; but adopting the Realist's detached standpoint, they presented their subject without criticism, emotion, or aestheticism. The Naturalists and later the Impressionists worked in this vein.

Toward the end of the third quarter of the century there were artists who began following the path indicated by Bonington and the English water-colorists, by Turner and Constable, by Delacroix and Courbet; in their vision and their manner of applying paint to the canvas in loose strokes they preserved the freshness of their reaction to a subject. Eugène Boudin (1824-98) made quick sketches of seashores and crowds in crinolines, or, in his marine scenes built up of quick, pulsating strokes, gave the atmosphere of sky and restlessness of water flickering in sunlight against the boats and docks. The Dutchman Johann Jongkind (1819-91), a friend of the Barbizon painters, sketched scenes similar to Boudin's against a more dramatic background.

Edouàrd Manet (1832-83), the genius of this generation, worked in a style quite different from those we have just noticed. He looked to Spain, and to Velasquez in particular, for his contrasting palette of blacks and silver grays with touches of high color. Manet flattened his figures into areas of paint, using such sparse halftones that their silhouettes contrasted sharply with negative backgrounds. He preferred the unrelieved contour of the human figure broken only by the details necessary to explain the essential forms. In his famous *Luncheon on the Grass* of 1863 the figures are carefully and impersonally posed, flatly silhouetted within the

1. Corot: *Ville d'Avray*. 1860.
Copyright: the Frick Collection, New York.

2. Millet: *The Gleaners*. 1857.
Louvre, Paris. (Giraudon)

frame of trees, and locked into a clearly defined pattern. As he went on, Manet loosened his style and dissipated the contours of his figures; in the end his quick and energetic brush was won over to Impressionism, a style he helped to create.

In mid-century England the ugliness and dislocation of life in a modern industrial civilization had begun to weigh heavily on a group of young painters. They looked romantically elsewhere and to other times (as had the Nazarenes in Germany or the Primitives in France) for what they believed was a simpler life, innocent faith, and guiding principles for a new art. These were the Pre-Raphaelites. The poet Dante Gabriel Rossetti (1828-82) in his painting evoked the spirit of Botticelli, to which he added a neurotic anxiety diffused in a vague and flowing style, as is his *Blessed Damosel*, inspired by Keats' medieval world. Edward Burne-Jones (1833-98) respected the masters of the late quattrocento in his tender renderings of personages from Greek myths or his frail and chaste heroes enacting the Quest of the Holy Grail. Others such as J. E. Millais (1829-96) in his original and literary subjects and W. Holman Hunt (1827-1910) with homely Biblical subjects described in sharp detail added to the fame of this group. Ford Madox Brown (1821-93) shared their ideas.

William Morris (1834-96) adapted the interest of the group to all the arts of daily living. Opposing the urban civilization that threatened to wipe out individual artisans whose craft had developed through the ages, he advocated a revival of medieval craftsmanship in an effort to check the vulgarity of cheap and profusely manufactured products. Christianity, socialism,

1. Mount: *Raffling for the Goose*. 1837.
Metropolitan Museum of Art, New York.
(Gift of J. D. Crimmins)

2. Durand: *Kindred Spirits*. 1849.
New York Public Library.

and aestheticism were to guide his followers to a world in which art should play the highest civilizing role; and John Ruskin (1819-1900), drawing on the Venetian Gothic and the Italian Early Renaissance, proposed in many volumes a credo of life, morality, and art for the Victorians.

In America Asher B. Durand (1796-1886) continued in his style of Romantic realism, leaning on "accurate drawing" and frank imitation, the Real being more important than the Ideal. From the green and palisaded vistas of the Hudson River to the vastness of the Far West native painters contemplated the awe-inspiring and sublime—described by such men as Friedrich in Germany and Turner, John Martin, and Francis Danby in England. On the eastern seaboard John Kensett (1816-72) excelled in atmospheric descriptions of mountains, fields, and seas; J. Cropsey, Robert Havell, and George Durrie recorded similar subjects. When he moved to the Far West Kensett adapted his brush to descriptions of the new landscape. Albert Bierstadt (1830-1902), attracted to the grandiose and fantastic of the vast pioneer country with its inspiring background of rugged mountain and romantic forests, recaptured the melodramatic spirit of Turner. Others remembered for this Rocky Mountain style are Worthington Whittredge, Thomas Moran, Sanford Gifford, and William Keith. The most outstanding in this group

1. Rossetti: *Beata Beatrix*.
1872. Art Institute of Chicago.
(Gift of C. L. Hutchinson)

2. Carpeaux: *La Danse*. 1869.
(Arch. Photo)

of aggressive panoramic painters was Frederick
Church (1826-1900), in vogue with his gigantic scenes
depicting everything from the grandeur of primeval
forest to the warmth of the Athenian Acropolis. The
influence of the Barbizon painters appeared in the canvases of William M. Hunt (1824-1879) and especially
in those of George Inness (1825-94), who in his later
years turned to a freer and more spontaneous inter-
pretation of nature. The genre tradition was continued
by such men as John Quidor, William S. Mount, George

Bingham, and Richard Woodville. Nathaniel Currier (1813-88) and James Ives (1824-95) in their popular lithographs became the active chroniclers of their generation.

Barye continued to sculpt his marvelous animals through the third quarter of the century, though in his *War* and *Peace* he vigorously turned to a classical theme of heroic groups. Jean-Baptiste Carpeaux (1827-75) produced work that characterized the ebullient spirit of the French Second Empire and prepared the ground for the great talents that were to mature at the end of the century. His portraits of the imperial family and of elegant women show a vibrant surface pocked with flickering lights animating enigmatic expressions; the portrait of Charles Garnier succeeds in rendering its subject's lively personality. His *Dance* for the Opéra pays homage to the great sculptors of the preceding century.

In architecture this last generation of eclectic builders relying on the thematic exuberances of the past, before the next generation will question such practices, had its great spokesman in Charles Garnier (1825-98). For the next fifty years he set the style of the acceptable and beautiful, more opulent and less elegant, for the reigning bourgeoisie. His Paris Opéra, a great eclectic splurge of past styles reappropriated, is dazzling and impressive; when Emperor Napoleon III asked him what the new style was to be called, he replied: Napoleon III. Around the traditional eighteenth-century opera house horseshoe the architect added a swooping flight of baroque stairs, a glittering foyer paneled with mirrors and ceilinged with paintings set in robust frames; corridors here and there lead to the great well of the staircase up which the eye moves restlessly along coupled pied-marble columns, pilasters, balustrades, balconies, and arches; gilt bronzes and mosaics, alabaster and precious materials all compete with each other to dizzy the spectator's senses. Inside the Opéra, rows of red plush alternate with horizontal golden movements of the encircling balconies, the whole space punctuated by the spreading chandelier swinging beneath a great painted dome. The massive front façade is clearly proportioned amid a wealth of architectural detail: a loggia with square openings grows from the arcaded entrance ornamented with sculpture groups (Carpeaux's *Dance* being one), the whole rising gravely to the monumental bronzes at either corner flanking a flattened dome crowned by Apollo and the Muses. The Opéra was later provided with a long avenue leading toward it, one of the spectacular settings of Baron Haussmann (1809-91), who in his sweeping realignment of the city arteries thought in terms of great boulevards moving toward glorious vistas of *monuments historiques*. Given ample powers, he moved the traffic of the expanding city along broad avenues, ruthlessly demolishing whatever stood in the way of thoroughfares. In his urban planning he solved some of the problems that congested cities are faced with, but in turn he created others. Many European capitals were influenced by his vision for a newly created modern city.

In the Paris of the 50's Visconti and Lefuel built extensive additions to the Louvre; the principal features of these were massive pavilions standing at intervals, between which the walls are recessed—except on the ground floor where a continuous arcaded gallery

Garnier: *Exterior of the Paris Opéra.* 1861-74. (Giraudon)

links them. The pavilions are accented by coupled columns bearing heavy volutes and an exuberant ornamentation of massed figures and architectural elements submerging the window of the mansard. This rich sculptural effect represents the ideal of Second-Empire architecture. Elsewhere in the city J. F. Duban in his Ecole des Beaux-Arts of 1860 (the institution that was to play an important part as the adversary of the Impressionists) used large rounded windows to emphasize the light that must function in the studios there, while

Garnier: *Interior of the Paris Opéra.* (Giraudon)

the interior generously divides space among court-yards, galleries, classrooms, and exhibition and administration rooms.

In London Barry's Houses of Parliament came to completion in 1865, a highly revered and much emulated architectural achievement. In Glasgow in the 50's Alexander Thomson's Caledonia Road Church employed massive rectangular units, a classic Greek temple with Ionic columns forming a decorative second story. A boldly proportioned bell tower rises along its rhythmical horizontal bands of walls, unbroken except briefly by severe openings at its summit. The austerity of its simply conceived plan and the clear interrelation of its parts are emphasized by flat surfaces and linear cornices defining the lines of the building without unduly protruding from it. This generation witnessed the slow construction of Joseph Poelaert's Law Courts, an ambitious monument to the eclecticism of several styles; in a massive summary of architectural vocabulary it manages to impose its awesome bulk through the overwhelming weight of monumental and decorative devices meant to impress by the heavy authority of its lumbering multifoliate parts. In the United States a classical efflorescence occurred in 1851-65 in Washington, D.C., as Thomas Walter added two wings to the Capitol and raised the central dome on a great colonnaded drum, completing in this way a cycle of architectural intention beginning in the early days of the Republic and continuing for well over fourscore years. A dignified neo-Renaissance then took its place in this city as Mullet and Gilman's State, War, and Navy Department Building in a neo-château style vied with neo-Gothic and neo-Romanesque styles. In straining to come to a definition of their intentions, architects created a unique nineteenth-century style, complicated as a wedding cake but reassuring and grandiose in proclamative façades and ostentatious ornamentation: a solution well suited to the tastes of a generation that felt this profusion was part of a Renaissance—as indeed it was, until a succeeding Renaissance was to challenge the formulas.

1. Barry : *Houses of Parliament, London.*
1840-65. (British Information Service)

2. U. S. Capitol. 1865.

4

IMPRESSIONISM
AND
OTHER SCHOOLS

1875-1900

Monet: *At the River*. 1868.
Art Institute of Chicago.
(H. and P. Palmer Collection)

■ Impressionism grew up alongside and out of the established schools of painters who exhibited their work in the official salon. In 1867—year of the great Paris world's fair, when Ingres died, a few years after Delacroix and Delaroche—Manet joined Courbet to defy the exclusiveness of this powerful salon with private (and unsuccessful) exhibitions of their own work; while the salon jury rejected the paintings submitted by Renoir, Monet, Sisley, Cézanne, Brazille and others. At this moment the members of the young group were already oriented to the new concepts evident in their first group exhibition of 1874. They were competing with recognized painters whose company they sought, painters whose styles were frankly derived from one of the three important schools mentioned: Gérôme's style from Ingres', Fromentin's from Delacroix's, and Meissonier's from Delaroche's "Golden Mean." These reputable masters considered themselves conscious heirs of the great traditions in painting; it was they who, with others, professors at the Ecole des Beaux-Arts or members of the Institut de France, sat on the salon juries to accept or reject the works submitted. The jury list for the Salon of 1867, a roster of those who had arrived at the apex of acceptability in art, shows in what milieu the Impressionists first moved: Cabanel, Pils, Gérôme, Fromentin, Baudry, T. Rousseau, J. Breton, Français, Meissonier, Couture, and

Gleyre (with whom many Impressionists studied) among the painters; in sculpture Dumont, Barye, and Guillaume; in architecture Labrouste, Lenoir, Duc, and Vaudoyer, to which the names of Lefuel, Viollet-le-Duc, and Ballu were added. Other names complete the list: Theodore Rousseau was the president of the painting section, Dumont of the sculpture, and Labrouste of the architecture. The president of all the sections combined was Nieuwerkerke, Courbet's great enemy. On the jury were also some museum curators, and writers such as Théophile Gautier and Charles Blanc, both strongly pro-Ingres critics. The jury members had fixed and definite standards for good art: *correct* drawing, appreciation of the *Juste Milieu*, respect for the traditional norms and forms, proper local color (the true color of the object), though some attenuated Delacroix brushwork might be allowed, inspiration from standard schools of past art, proper subjects without vulgarity and with high seriousness and nobility. To this might be added: a style derived from a respectable teacher willing to vouch for the integrity and talent of the young painter. Naturally enough, the new young aspirants found it difficult to meet with this strict official approval. In 1863 the jury had rejected so many works that the Emperor Napoleon III authorized a separate salon for the disgruntled, to be called the Salon des Réfusés (of the Refused). Manet, Pissarro, Jongkind, Fantin-Latour, Whistler, Cézanne, and others were among those who submitted works there. But the Emperor was displeased with the results of the exhibition and made no provision for another. Young painters had no recourse but to attempt to be accepted by the salon jury, whose approval meant success and commissions. Buyers of art were interested in official salon painters. Baudry painted his expensive murals for the great princes, bankers, and courtesans, and for the Paris Opéra in a pleasing and colorful pictorial late eighteenth-century Venetian style; Bouguereau and Cabanel exhibited the same nudes as Courbet, but theirs were idealized and proper and not realist; Gérôme did ambitious Delacroix scenes in an Ingres technique, while Fromentin also watered down the great Romantic; Gleyre carried on the Ingres tradition in a Delaroche way, while Meissonier was pure Delaroche done in miniature; Carolus-Duran asserted himself as a great portrait painter, Renaissance manner. Landscape being a safe subject, the Barbizon school was enormously popular. Not all these approved painters were hostile to the newcomers: Rousseau was sympathetic and there were others. But in the main the jury guarded carefully the sacred precincts of what they held to be tradition and respectability. In it we also find advanced men such as Labrouste in architecture and Barye in sculpture; and this must be said in its favor: the salons were international enough in scope to include such names as Alma-Tadema, Frith, Landseer, and Leighton from England, for example, or Winterhalter and Kaulbach from Germany; the Swiss Gleyre and the Dutch Jongkind participated, as well as others from Italy, Russia, and the United States. Many of these men made their reputation through the salons.

The early work of the Impressionist painters did not depart far from the norms of the salon painting, but they soon moved further away, and in 1874 decided to hold their own exhibition in the studio of the photog-

Gleyre: *Lost Illusions.* 1843.
Louvre, Paris. (Arch. Photo)

rapher Nadar. Monet, Renoir, Degas, Cézanne, and
Berthe Morisot exhibited paintings; salon-conscious
Manet remained aloof. At their second exhibition the
following year Pissarro and others joined. These ven-
tures were not successful and the salon, for which these
young radicals still yearned, did not suffer and perhaps was strengthened by them. It was fifteen years
before the new movement made itself felt; and when
the salon at last reacted, the movement had splintered
or become transformed into something else.

The source of this new style must be sought in those
old masters using a broad and large touch: Tintoretto,

Carolus-Duran: *Countess Pourtalès*. 1873.
Private Collection, Paris. (Arch. Photo)

Hals, Goya, Velásquez, Delacroix, Turner, Constable;
late Titian, El Greco, Rembrandt, eighteenth-century
painters in France and Italy. The Impressionists were
drawn to a freer, open brushwork where the quality
of the paint was evident, the bravura and the touch of
the brushwork important. They were drawn to color
and colorists, and rather than mixing their color on
their palettes they preferred placing pure color stroke
beside stroke on their canvas, so that at a distance the
juxtaposition merged in the eye. Claude Monet (1840-
1926) painted *plein air* (outdoor) subjects, setting his
canvas in the open air and describing the people and

Bouguereau: *The Bathers*. 1884.
Art Institute of Chicago. (A. D. Munger Collection)

places he knew. A friend of Boudin, he attempted to capture the spontaneity of vision immersed in light and bright shadow, the life of the inanimate world woven into the tissue of changing sunlight, as in his great series on Rouen cathedral. Apart from the subject it depicts, Monet's paint has an existence in itself; each touch, rather than the scene which is the pretense for the work, asserts itself as his real object. This is especially true of his *Nymphéas* and his late work where the details of the painting are concrete and abstract at the same time, the objects setting the scene while the brush strokes act it out. Camille Pissarro (1830-1903) in his Impressionist manner is similar to the early Monet, preserving the form that might otherwise trickle away in the little spots of light flickering over his canvases; later, influenced by Pointillism and the discoveries of other painters, he changed his style. Alfred Sisley (1839-99) in his scenes of the Seine valley continued the early Impressionist manner, as did Berthe Morisot (1841-95) and Eva Gonzalès (1849-83) in their vivid descriptions of domestic life.

Auguste Renoir (1841-1919) for a time shared the view of his fellow-painters, but was drawn to the eighteenth century (which had once served him for the porcelains and fans he had painted in his youth) and to the Delacroix tradition of bright color freely applied. Having studied Ingres' *Madame Rivière,* he journeyed to Italy in 1881 and discovered Raphael, Ingres' source. Feeling that Impressionism concentrated on effect at the expense of form, he changed, for the next fifteen years, to an Ingrist style; from these years come his monumental women bathers, large placid areas of flesh color contained within an all-embracing

contour, with the human figure emphatic and the background diffused with flowing Impressionist brush strokes. Toward the end of the century, fingers crippled by arthritis and brushes strapped to his hands, he simplified generous female nudes while his palette turned to rose, vermilion, red, and every variety of warm living color. A sensuous artist who liked painting and sculpture for themselves, he painted with a large physical appetite for the labor of creating.

Edgar Degas (1834-1917), taught by an Ingres student, wanted to do large history paintings and was attracted to the superiority of line vaunted by old Ingres. Even during his Impressionist adherence Degas could not forego line—an attitude ostensibly at variance

with the new tenets. Unlike his Impressionist colleagues, Degas would not admit the value of *plein-air*
painting; he felt it was better to paint from memory
a subject transformed by imagination; in the atelier
one could conjure up the exterior atmosphere. His work
is the most literary of all, for he used a modern sentiment to describe his time. This led him to a sort of
naturalism, where reality was identified with all its
accidental ironies and bitter pettinesses. Here the
painter makes no comment, though his personages do:
boredom, indifference, hostility, and apathy move
through his figures; gestures of fatigue creep into the
ballerina's arabesque. Degas, interested in composition
(not the unposed and haphazard scenes his friends ad-

vocated), carefully built up elements in his work along new lines. He resorted to a photographic technique which, by arbitrarily cutting the scene, suggests its extension into the world around the picture space. In the Japanese manner he often sees his scenes from a plunging perspective, the dominant compositional element placed at the periphery or even cut by the frame, while a diagonal perspective abruptly moves the scene away from the spectator. Degas' interest in people is transformed in late pastels: through the use of broken lines and hatching he can reduce the portrait to a still life with no animation but the excitement of an un-

usually composed picture. As a sculptor too, especially in the medium of wax studies (many cast in bronze today), he caught the instantaneous and intimate actions of his favorite subjects.

The Impressionists often shocked the bourgeoisie not only by their manner of painting loosely, brokenly, and disjointedly, but in their choice of subject matter or rather in their casual attitude toward it: Manet painted *Nana,* a young courtesan dressing while her gentleman friend waits tiredly nearby; Degas showed intimate scenes of women having their toenails pared or washing and drying themselves in anything but classical tubs.

Renoir: *Les Grandes Baigneuses.* 1887.
Philadelphia Museum of Art.
(Mrs. Carroll Tyson Collection)

1. Degas: *Dancer*. 1878.
Louvre, Paris. (Bulloz)

2. Renoir: *On the Terrace*. 1881.
Art Institute of Chicago.
(Mr. and Mrs. Lewis L. Coburn Collection)

2

Degas: *The Tub*. About 1886.
Metropolitan Museum of Art, New York.
(H. O. Havemeyer Collection)

Scenes of low-life and personal life were acceptable, but only if properly and discreetly rendered and idealized—something Degas would never consent to. The artist took great freedom with his subject matter especially in France; and every new generation had to do something really daring to shock the bourgeoisie, which after each decade had managed to absorb the previous shock.

Most of the Impressionists were making their way by 1890. There was one exception: Paul Cézanne (1839-1906), whose original and great contribution to art was not evident until some time later. His fellow-artists were involved with the transitory spectacle of daily events momentarily imprisoned in light and shade, and Cézanne disliked the impermanence of their results. Though he belonged to their group for a few years, exhibiting his work alongside theirs, he knew his path lay elsewhere. Cézanne, interested in structure and well-balanced compositions, planned his paintings so that all details relate to one another. To achieve this, he created his own undiminishing perspective, his backgrounds not attenuated by distance. Distance and foreground equal partners in a stable composition, Cézanne's timeless space now moved back and forth in planes composed of small areas of color enhanced by consorting lines. The painter's sense of the permanent was drawn from an immemorial "geology" moving through the mountains and still lifes he painted, while he thought in terms of "cosmic prisms" and the "infinite." To accentuate this tragic and relentless motion in things that were themselves motionless, he further disrupted the edges of the planes, whose disjointed contours appear unfulfilled as they struggle to complete themselves in the profiles of his fruit or his tabletops and mountainsides.

Cézanne did not model but modulated, as he said, not with shadow but with hatched lines of color that push the form nervously flat as much as they keep it rounding away from our eyes. He never hesitated to take the world of three-dimensional space and warp it like a pliable sheet of copper, so that the third dimension is forced back into the second in order to satisfy the compositional pattern the painter had set up. And as is the case in Japanese art, the spectator is endowed with unusual vision as his line of sight not only touches the side of the jar but may bend and enter the jar itself. In his attempt to simplify this vision, Cézanne felt that nature could be reduced to such geometrical elements as the cylinder, sphere, and cone, shapes providing simple common denominators for forms in nature. It was not in his own time but in the twentieth century that Cézanne's precepts for the creation of an

art work were to be most influential.

Others affiliated somehow with Impressionist painters added their individual note. Armand Guillaumin and Albert André painted landscapes and interiors with bright colors surging through simplified compositions. Henri Moret and Gustave Loiseau often suggest Monet and Pissarro in seascapes, as does Maufra; Lebourg in attenuated river scenes shrouded in atmosphere and Lépine in suffused views of Montmartre are more original. There are also such pseudo-Impressionists as interesting Henri Martin working with a Barbizon theme, and other curious painters such as Albert Besnard and Gaston Latouche depicting a fashionable world of leisurely women. And even in the twentieth century later Impressionists such as Henri Lebasque show pleasant and attractive styles.

The Impressionists had many friends, imitators, and adherents from other countries. Among these, the Philadelphian Mary Cassatt (1845-1926) won praise from Degas, who influenced her work. Her subjects were drawn mainly from events in her own personal and feminine circle in France: outings with friends, teas, mothers caring for children, people sitting ornamentally through a long afternoon. She was an excellent pastellist and a gifted printmaker, imitating the Japanese in one of her successful series. She also helped

1. Sargent: *Madame Gautreau*. 1884.
Metropolitan Museum of Art, New York.

2. Homer: *Croquet Scene*. 1866.
Art Institute of Chicago.
(Friends of American Art Collection)

3. Cassatt: *Young Mother Sewing*. 1903.
Metropolitan Museum of Art, New York
(H. O. Havemeyer Collection)

popularize the work of her fellow-artists and encouraged the acquisition of fine works by them that now form the nucleus of many an American museum collection. Her compatriot James Whistler (1834-1903) had studied with Gleyre and painted with Fantin-Latour, a lyrical artist who preserved forms while evaporating them in a sweet semi-Impressionist palette; later Whistler painted with Courbet. He went his own way after that, respecting always the subject before him but attempting to render it in terms he called "harmonies," the color patterns and separate intensities creating islands within the painting that reverberate to each other; he tunes the details in his work so that the pitch is perfect, down to the last overtone or insignificant element on his canvas. Sometimes he called his paintings symphonies or nocturnes to enforce in the mind of the spectator their pervasive moods. An excellent and productive printmaker, a penetrating portraitist, and an engaging conversationalist, he affected Symbolist painting during his lifetime.

Another American, John S. Sargent (1856-1925), shows some Impressionist influence in his water colors, though he is remembered for his dazzling portraits with their sure bravura touch, a technique employed by the fashionable Italian Giovanni Boldini and the Swedish Anders Zorn. In England Walter Sickert (1860-1942) was attracted to the Impressionist technique, which he developed into a free and personal style. Other Europeans were attracted to the prevailing or later form of the Impressionist idiom: the Germans Max Liebermann and Max Slevogt, the Dutch Ten Cate, the Spaniard Sorolla y Bastida, the Italians Fattori, Signorini, Segantini, and Zandomeneghi. In the United States

Childe Hassam and John Twachtman worked in this idiom, though here other men made a greater contribution in other styles: Thomas Eakins (1844-1916), with a penetrating realism, engrossing Winslow Homer (1836-1910) who adds a romantic freshness of vision; Albert F. Ryder (1847-1917) with a mystical symbolism; William M. Harnett (1848-92) with his *trompe l'oeil* pre-Surrealist still lifes.

In 1886, the year of the last Impressionist exhibition, the Neoimpressionists made their appearance. Also called Pointillists and Divisionists, they clarified and systematized the practices of their predecessors. Paul Signac (1863-1935), the theoretician for the new group, described the method of painting: careful and structured compositions were to be created from rectangular dashes of color purposely contrasting with their complementary neighbors; and by the law of simultaneous contrast the dark tones were to be vitalized by light touches and vice versa. The color theories of Chevreul, Helmholtz, and Rood helped him in his dogma; though it was hard to proceed with exact science, and Signac succeeded best as an uncautious watercolorist. To these theories Georges Seurat (1859-95) added those of Fechner on the use of the harmonious rectangle. From Lehmann, an Ingres student, he had inherited a sense for monumental history painting; from his Impressionist predecessors, a penchant for bright colors. With these things in mind he built up his poetically mechanical world. *Sunday Afternoon on La Grande Jatte,* the most successful of his paintings, is no casual relaxed impression but the result of endless preparatory sketches, in the tradition of classical history painting. Forms moving parallel to the picture frame recede in

1. Whistler: *Old Battersea Bridge, Nocturne—Blue and Gold.* 1865. Tate Gallery, London. (British Information Service)

2. Eakins: *Max Schmitt in a Single Scull.* 1871. Metropolitan Museum of Art, New York.

measured relation to similarly placed forms, down to the picture's horizon, the scene rising across the canvas to create a "happy" painting, as Seurat intended it. The bright pigment vibrates harmoniously in this classically balanced work where all the carefully calculated parts sum up to an immobile and timeless serenity.

It was possible to be an innovator in this period without being an Impressionist, as was the case of Whistler and Fantin-Latour. Puvis de Chavannes (1824-98) continued in the Ingres tradition; inspired by sentiment, religion, and poetry, he became highly successful in the seventies with his large mural paintings that so admirably adhere to and accompany architectural spaces. He was admired by Gauguin and Seurat; and Toulouse-Lautrec even copied his *Sacred Wood,* though he caricatured it too. Some painters, picking up the intuitive and inspired thread running through Romanticism, turned to the inner world of

dream- or literature-filled imagination, rather than to the outer world reflected in the eye. Drawing on the rich and varied heritage which included Baudelaire, Gautier, Rimbaud, and Poe (translated into French by Baudelaire and admired by Mallarmé, the most influential of the late-century poets), Gustave Moreau (1826-98) furbished out his canvases with grandiose and never-finished pictorial dreams, as gaudy and jewel-decked as the visions in Oscar Wilde's *Salomé* or Huysmans' *Against the Grain*. Odilon Redon (1840-1916), guided by the botanist Clavaud, searched among the marine, terrestrial, uterine, and astral mysteries of life where phantasmagoric creatures pursue us with their "visual logic" in scintillating pastel colors or glowing black and white. Redon is the precursor of those who paint from the subconscious, a pre-Surrealist; and his world of animal and floral life, his mythologies of Venus and Pegasus have a dreamlike

Seurat: *Sunday Afternoon on the Island of La Grande Jatte.* 1884-86. Art Institute of Chicago. (Helen Birch Bartlett Collection)

1. Toulouse-Lautrec: *La Clownesse*. 1895.
Louvre, Paris. (Arch. Photo)

2. Vuillard: *Public Garden*. 1894.
Museum of Modern Art, Paris. (Arch. Photo)

1

A PORTFOLIO
OF MASTERPIECES
IN COLOR

David: *Portrait of Madame Récamier*. (Detail). 1800.
Louvre, Paris.

Delacroix: *Nude Sitting*. 1824.
Louvre, Paris.

Manet: *The Fifer*. 1866.
Louvre, Paris.

Degas: *Portrait of a Young Lady*. 1867.
Louvre, Paris.

Seurat: *Nude*. 1887. Louvre, Paris.

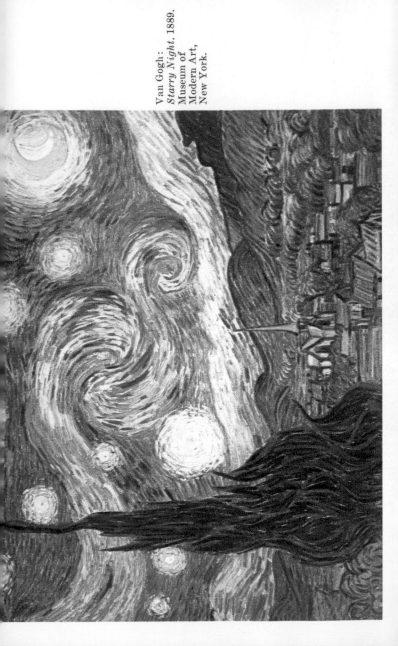

Van Gogh:
Starry Night. 1889.
Museum of
Modern Art,
New York.

Gauguin:
Nave Nave Moe.
1894.
Hermitage,
Leningrad.

Monet: *Water Lilies*. 1904.
Louvre, Paris.

Rousseau: *The Snake Charmer*. 1907.
Louvre, Paris.

Redon: *Wild Flowers*. 1912. Louvre, Paris.

Braque: *The Guitar Player*. 1917.
Kunstmuseum, Basel.

Kandinsky: *Black Spot*. 1921.
Kunsthaus, Zurich.

Picasso: *The Lovers.* 1923.
National Gallery of Art, Washington.

Chagall: *The Lovers on the Roof*. 1927-28.
Musées Royaux Des Beaux-Arts, Brussels.

persuasiveness presented with masterly draughtsman-
ship and an extraordinary sense of color.

The notions of the Symbolist poets and painters, pro-
pounded by Albert Aurier (idea is inherent in the
form; the synthesized forms are written in signs that
exalt decorative, emotive, and mystic elements), influenced Paul Gauguin (1848-1903). In Brittany he
gathered about him a sect known as the Synthetists.
Feeling that "art is an abstraction" and guided by
Egyptian and Giottesque models, Gauguin flattened his
figures, simplified the drawing, and emphasized the
decorative surface in a flat two-dimensional and large-
patterned way. His *Yellow Christ* shows his appreciation of the emotive value of color and the primitive
qualities of medieval art in picturesque Brittany. In
1891 he left for Tahiti, elaborating there his mysterious
and monumental vision and maturing the literary and
symbolic elements of his canvas. His simplified forms
and dramatic large-cut patterns lent themselves to an

unusual series of color woodcuts. On his flattened surfaces he often used colors that drew their validity not
from the objects they represent but from their function in the all-over decorative patterns that surge
through the composition.

Gauguin fled from isolation in contemporary civilization to loneliness in the midst of Tahitian nature; but
he had briefly believed in a community of artists working together in medieval fashion, a belief that Vincent
Van Gogh (1853-90) had attempted to put into practice. Van Gogh began by following the path of Daubigny, Delacroix, Mauve, and Israels, painting in a
dark and distorted mood the Belgium miners amongst
whom he had evangelized. Moving to Paris, he discovered the dazzling light of the Impressionist palette
and the meaning of color. In the south of France his
subjects move from bright fields and houses, conceived

1. Van Gogh: *Night Café*, 1888-89.
Yale University Art Gallery.
(Stephen S. Clark Collection)

2. Gauguin: *Ia Orana Maria*. 1891.
Metropolitan Museum of Art, New York.
(Bequest of Samuel A. Lewisohn)

IA ORANA MARIA

in terms of pure color and large brush strokes, to the morbid *Night Café*, a place "to ruin oneself, run mad or commit a crime"; there in the lamplit scene somber greens and reds evoke the terror and harshness of evil. Like Gauguin, with whom he worked for a short while in Arles in 1890, Van Gogh set down many of his ideas, so that we are aware of his extraordinary intentions. Exulting in the generous and glowing sun-fevered world, Van Gogh attributed to the elements of the natural world, to color and line, the same emotions that urged him to paint, so that each corner of his canvas was moved by a powerful inner urge. The forces that sharpen nature to an anguished awareness are interpreted in terms of the suffering and uneasiness that the painter felt; he has permeated the canvas not with the subject but with himself and his own persuasive feelings. This undetached attitude is no longer Impressionism but Expressionism; for the painter has a compelling point of view, a decided emotion, distorting the subject until it becomes for the spectator but a manifestation of that emotion.

Manet and Degas also moved beyond the attempted visual objectivity of Impressionism; their direction differs from Van Gogh's, however; they may be considered as sharers in the principles of Naturalism, an outgrowth of Courbet's Realism, which pretended to be an amoral, detached, and impartial attitude to all aspects of life. Since the ugly, the banal, and the brutal force us to face reality, we can show how impartial we are by representing them—even though any pleasant subject will do too. Naturalism was the banner of the famous novelist Emile Zola, who furnished several themes for Manet and Renoir. Henri de Toulouse-

Lautrec (1864-1901), influenced by Degas, found Degas' Naturalism so congenial that he cherished it long after the idealist-symbolists had taken the field; but he made more brutal, ugly, cruel, and terrifying all the mild Naturalist elements he found. Critical and bitter, he gathered all the desparate facts of sordidness, human degradation, and despair (so terrible that they are beyond remedy) for the substance of his waking nightmares. Like many of his contemporaries he preferred flat arabesques of form moving freely against neutral backgrounds, a procedure highly successful in his famous posters and his thinly painted portraits on cardboard. He exaggerated, all but caricatured, everything he saw, and selected subject matter principally from the world of theater, circus, and prostitution to project the mask of ironic comedy and tragedy. But in investing his forms with an eloquence of their own, emphasizing the spontaneous patterns within his composition and increasing the rhythmic beat of his idea, he emerged eventually with a fascinating symbolism that he shared with many of his contemporaries.

With Gauguin's departure Paul Sérusier had become the propagandist of the Symbolists, known in 1889 as the Nabis (or Prophets), a group which included such men as Denis, Bonnard, and Vuillard. In general they found their subjects in the very ordinary life of the bourgeoisie surrounding them: wife, children, parents, uncles, aunts, and friends; a stream of interior and exterior scenes flowed from their brushes showing the well-ordered and agreeable life of France's Third Republic. They enlarged on themes inherited from such artists as Renoir and Berthe Morisot and domesticated the whole vocabulary of painting. Their

note is *douceur de vivre* (comfort of living) presented
with nostalgia. Edouard Vuillard (1868-1940) in the
beginning worked with large abstract forms echoing
those of Gauguin, though in time these gave way to
fussy yet tastefully arranged domestic interiors, seen
through the medium of pastel or oil, in which the
figures are embedded as though sharing the patterns
of their décor. As he worked through the twentieth
century he became somewhat repetitious. Pierre Bonnard (1867-1947) was more interested in the potentials
of his canvas's surface than in the subjects he casually
arranged to elaborate it; his decorative panels done in
the Japanese style of his Symbolist days give way at
the turn of the century to canvases where shadowless
figures breathe in an atmosphere of vibrant flat color:
his is an effortless world of relaxed figures in summer
landscapes and gentle nudes in interiors rendered often
with a dry and crisp gouache technique. Maurice Denis
(1870-1943) used similar flat ornamental patterns for
themes often religious and historical, Neoclassical and
Neo-Ingrist, commissioned as decorations for public
buildings. Vuillard's brother-in-law Roussel preferred
to represent middle-class afternoons of fauns. Vallot-
ton, Ranson, and Verkade offered other individual
notes.

Young artists who came to France were often im-

1. Munch: *The Shriek*.
Lithograph, 1895.
Peter Deitz Collection.

2. Frémiet: *Gorilla
Carrying off Savage*. 1895.
Zoo, Paris. (Giraudon)

pressed with the current Parisian movement, incorporating it on first impact into their native style. Edvard Munch (1863-1944), affected first by the Naturalism he discovered in Paris in 1885, absorbed in time the Symbolist and Nabis doctrine: his *Moonlight* of 1893 owes much to Gauguin. His real contribution to art became apparent the following year in his *Anguish*, which announces a long series of studies of psychological states of mind during moments of terror or despair, in sickness or death. Tinged with a literary flavor, the anguish of these emotional states is expressed by the webs of linear movement swirling and trapping his figures. Like his paintings, his series of lithographs are preoccupied with emotional tragedy. At about the same time James Ensor (1860-1949) worked in Belgium in a rather attenuated Impres-

sionist manner, interpreting with a kind of Expressionist-Symbolist intent masks and dolls, crowds and tête-à-têtes; his vision of the "exquisite turbulence" of life, as revealed by his *Entry of Christ into Brussels* of 1888, is a mysterious masquerade of emotions under a "*somptueux décor.*" Others, such as the Swiss Hodler, a monumental colorist defining his shapes in terse linear outlines, and Arnold Böcklin, reveling in the mysterious bacchanales of nymphs and neriads in the wan light of strange afternoons, continue in a different tradition. Elsewhere Dutchman Johannes Toorop and the fabulous and imaginative Aubrey Beardsley worked in a large flowing style that prepared the way for the new movement called Art Nouveau.

At this time European painters were becoming more interested in the primitive arts of all countries. Naive painter Henri Rousseau (1844-1910) painted mysterious scenes, real and imagined, where ordinary or exotic figures in profile or fullface are flattened into cardboard planes and enframed in meticulous foliage. Rhythmical in repeating forms and patterned detail, his landscapes and spellbound figures show a vigorous directness in their simplifications; they stimulated later painters seeking to sharpen the immediate visual appeal of their subjects.

During the last quarter of the century sculpture was not as inventive as painting; for one thing, sculpture was continually involved with its own tradition, and antique classical works had never lost their validity as an enduring achievement in the creative arts. Other influential traditions were those of the Italian Renaissance and the eighteenth century; a practicing sculptor looked back to these. By the middle of the century a new style which closely paralleled Realism became a kind of three-dimensional photographic realism with *la femme* as its subject. Sculptors kept close to the norm of the human body, the great theme in their art. There were none the less several who made a personal contribution to the history of their time. With Jules Dalou (1838-1902) a free realism was tempered by the example of Carpeaux's eighteenth-century verve in portrait contours; a liberal, he helped organize the Salon of the Dissidents in 1890. Jean Falguière (1831-1900), with such others as Henri Chapu, enjoyed much success with an honest realism, interpreting Diana as a *Parisienne* of her time and surcharging Paris with great bronze monuments. When the officials found Rodin's *Balzac* unacceptable, it was to Falguière they turned for a monument more suited to their taste. Emmanuel

1. Falguière: *Baroness Daumesnil*.
1879. Bonnat Museum,
Bayonne. (Arch. Photo)

2. Dalou: *The Peasant*.
1898. Louvre, Paris.
(Arch. Photo)

Rodin: *Monument to Balzac.* 1897.
Paris. (Giraudon)

Rosso: *The Concierge*. 1883.
Collection Museum of Modern Art, New York.

Frémiet (1824-1910), an exceptional sculptor haunted by prehistory and zoology, added to the sometimes bizarre production of the era with his predatory gorillas, charging elephants, and prowling centaurs.

Auguste Rodin (1840-1917) towered among the sculptors of this generation, though it remained for the next generation to discover that he had done so. In 1875, shortly after a trip to Florence where he discovered Michelangelo and Donatello, so important for the formation of his art, he produced his *Age of Bronze*. Though judged severely as a realist work cast from an actual human model, it won the sculptor a commission for the portals of the Museum of Decorative Arts; the resulting work was *The Gate of Hell*. In time Rodin's style became more complex as the sculptor defined his ideas on his art. To the realistic Beaux Arts and sturdy Italian traditions he grafted his own personal vision of palpitating surfaces over which fine light is broadly distributed; to this he soon added an impression which diffuses the light and creates a *sfumato* effect, similar to that achieved by his friend Eugène Carrière in painting. In Rodin's great *Gate* the Michelangelo tradition prevails, the placid surfaces knotted up and the figures flexed and postured into every conceivable kind of *contraposto*. This work took him to the end of the century. In its heavily charged symbolism it is on speaking terms with work by Gauguin's group, though Rodin was not interested in their kind of flat decorative relief. The exaggerated and literary style of the sculptor helps in the dramatic effects of sudden cavities of darkness poised dangerously against knobs of light, and in his *Balzac* conflicting simplified forms contrived out of the large defining sockets of shadow enact the great tragedy of the Olympian writer who reels imperviously away from the spectator.

Other interesting sculptors are Vicenzo Gemito (1852-1929) in his scrambling Neapolitan gamins and sensitive portraits where sketchy mobile surfaces animate the vital contours, similar to Carpeaux's; and Medardo Rosso (1858-1928), friend of Rodin, in his *Yvette Guilbert* revealing a summarizing technique close to late Manet, and his *Sick Child* with a soft Impressionist Carrière glaze heightening the pathos of the subject. In Belgium Constantin Meunier (1831-1905), preoccupied with the lives of miners, concerned himself with moving social themes akin to those in Van Gogh's Borinage paintings. In the United States a simplified Beaux-Arts tradition prevailed, as seen in the work of Augustus Saint-Gaudens (1848-1907): restrained and in good taste, his statue to General Sherman effects an admirable rapport with its surroundings.

In architecture new forms continued to be developed. International exhibitions offered a timely opportunity for the adaptation of new material to contemporary construction. The Paris fair of 1889 employed steel in an ostentatious and daring manner. In the Hall of Machines engineer Contamin and architect Dutert employed immense steel arches to emphasize an ample space enclosed by glass walls and roof. Gustave Eiffel (1832-1923), aided by engineers Koechlin and Nougier, conceived a high pointed tower rising on four sprawling legs, exploiting the new medium's capacity to rise and expand structurally in all directions. To solve the problem of wind pressure Eiffel used his system of openwork girders in his Douro Bridge of 1875 and Garabit Viaduct of 1879. Historian and critic Viollet-le-Duc championed an architecture employing iron, a medium visible in two Paris churches: Louis-Auguste Boileau's Saint-Eugène in 1854-55 and Victor Baltard's Saint-Augustin in 1860-61.

In the United States Henry Hobson Richardson (1838-86), formed by English and French traditions, worked in a revised Romanesque idiom of great arches and massive stone walls in college dormitories, churches, libraries, administration buildings, and railroad stations. The Marshall Field Wholesale Store of 1885-7 displayed monumental walls broken by win-

1

2

dows grouped doubly and triply within an ample round arch; its plain disposition of masonry contributed to establishing a mode for industrial architecture. With his death, his former assistants C. F. McKim and W. R. Mead (joined later by the imaginative Stanford White), abandoned this Romanesque vision in favor of one immersed in historical European styles.

In the great spurt of building activity after the Chicago fire of 1871 the Chicago architects developed still further the tall office buildings necessary in an expanding industrial era, gradually expressing the role of the steel skeleton in the contour of the façade. William LeBaron Jenney (1832-1907) introduced the skyscraper construction in his ten-story Home Life

1. *The Eiffel Tower*. 1887-89. Paris. (Arch. Photo)

2. Adler and Sullivan: *Wainwright Building*, St. Louis, Mo. 1890-1891. (Photo Museum of Modern Art, New York)

3. Richardson: *Marshall Field Building*. Chicago. 1885-87. (Photo Museum of Modern Art, New York)

3

Insurance Building of 1883-5; he trained William Holabird and Martin Roche who in their Tacoma Building of 1887-9 and later ones refined his system of masonry resting on a steel skeleton so that the skeleton is expressed in the exterior covering.

Aware of the work of Jenney and his group, Louis Henry Sullivan (1856-1924) with Dankmar Adler (aided by their young draftsman Frank Lloyd Wright) built the Chicago Auditorium Building in 1887-9, a complex edifice in a Richardsonian style with flattened masonry walls and with elaborate interior decoration inspired perhaps by Morris and Viollet-le-Duc. The firm of Sullivan and Adler next turned to their first skyscraper construction in the Saint Louis Wainwright

Building of 1890-1: the main elements of the steel skeleton are echoed by continuous vertical piers of brick; wide windows on the ground story indicate the distance between the skeletal supports; at the top, the piers suggest incipient capitals. A rich ornament moves around the attic windows and over the spandrels between piers and contrasts with the flat projecting cornice and the unadorned piers of the building's corners. In the Buffalo Guaranty Building of a few years later this scheme is further elaborated and extended as the ground floor frankly reveals the piers bearing the weight of the building. Designed by Sullivan in 1899, the Carson, Pirie and Scott Department Store in Chicago adds another note: the horizontal sweep of the construction replaces the former vertical one, contrasting with rising columns of the rounded pavilion at the corner; the wide Chicago windows clearly echo the steel skeleton. In many of these buildings a curvilinear vegetal decoration supplies an inventive and personal note.

In England a similar activity appeared in the construction of "commercial palaces" rising alongside traditional and authoritative Victorian Gothic London monuments such as Scott's Albert Memorial of 1863-72 and Street's Law Courts of the next decade. Other men invoked English tradition in a fresh way. In 1859 Philip Webb, favorite architect of the Pre-Raphaelite painters, built for William Morris and his wife The Red House at Bexley Heath in Kent. Of plain red brick and with no sculptural detail, the building shows a new spirit in its informality and the freedom of its plan. The exterior is unpretentious and uncluttered; the interior, a new monastic Gothic providing long and unadorned stretches of wall. In London Richard Norman Shaw (1831-1912) constructed his 1888 Queen's Gate House with a plain brick façade symmetrically arranged in an ordered manner of a Queen Anne style— a style his former partner William Eden Nesfield also admired. More advanced painters preferred architect Edward Godwin (1833-86), who in 1878 built Whistler's White House on Tite Street in London. The conception here is linear and delicate; the walls are painted white, doors and windows asymmetrically arranged on its white façade. Outside and inside, a Japanese simplicity prevails, as in the décor of this sparsely furnished house with its bare floors and plain walls. Goodwin also decorated Oscar Wilde's house nearby in the same fastidious manner.

Architects—designers of furniture, wallpaper, and chintzes as well—A. H. Mackmurdo (1851-1942) and Charles Voysey (1857-1941) are important for their achievement. In Mackmurdo's 1883 house in Enfield the second story relies for its effects on broad horizontal windows between flat uninterrupted bands and a simple roof. His influence is apparent in Voysey's 1891 London studio in the crisp horizontality of the parts and the clear grouping of doors and windows. Outstanding is Voysey's airy and light conception of interior decoration, as in The Orchard in Hertfordshire in 1900 with painted white woodwork, light blue tiles,

3

1. Webb: *The Red House at Bexley Heath*. Kent.
1859. (National Buildings Record)

2. Mackintosh: *School of Art, Glasgow*.
1897-9. (T. and R. Annan)

3. Godwin: *White House on Tite Street*. London.
1878-9. (National Buildings Record)

and open wooden grid shielding the staircase — the whole interior etched in the slim and elegant lines characteristic of Voysey's furniture and household utensils.

In Scotland Charles Mackintosh (1868-1928) improvised freely on this tradition in his 1897-9 Glasgow School of Art, its façade of large rectangular windows asserted in a flat frame of wall; the school's library wing of a decade later is more complex and dynamic as it rises aggressively from its sloping terrain. While this work looks forward to dynamic architects such as Sant'Elia, his 1897-8 Cranston Tea Room in Glasgow, revealing in a simple and delicate décor the sensuous elegance of its designer, was admired on the continent and impressed Art Nouveau movements in Vienna and elsewhere.

The spirit of Art Nouveau moved through many of the projects of this age. Art Nouveau, a style observable in painting as well as every other creative activity of the period, has its source in a number of things: Gothic, Chinese, and Japanese art, eighteenth-century Rococo, Symbolist and Expressionist painters and designers. Modeled on nature's large and generous swirling vegetal forms, this style patterns out leaflike into spirals and curves, waves and fringes. Its forms are reminiscent of those found in the paintings of Seurat and Gauguin, in designs by Mackmurdo and others. Its fevrile curvilinearity appears in the work of Beardsley, Toorop, and Klimt, and in the spiraling vegetal motif in Sullivan's architectural ornament.

The Art Nouveau style is characterized clearly in the Tassel House of 1892-3 in Brussels; here architect Victor Horta (1861-1947) drew freely on a curvilinear

Gaudí: *Sagrada Familia, Barcelona.*
1884-1914; 1919—. (Archivo Foto)

1. Horta: *Stairway,*
Tassel House, Brussels. 1892.

2. Gallé: *Vase.* Collection Corning Museum of Glass.
(Gift of Astrid Varnay)

impulse that embraced the whole interior decoration from the iron columns to the ubiquitous floral motifs of railings and floors. The Belgian Henri Van de Velde (1863-1957) spread the style in such early works as the capricious interior of the Haby barber shop in Berlin in 1901 and the designs for Samuel Bing's Paris shop specializing in objects in the new style. Hector Guimard (1867-1942) remains famous for his Paris subway entrances with their green arabesque forms unfolding upward like yearning vegetation. In Barcelona Antonio Gaudí (1852-1926) employed broken tiles and old pieces of crockery in the sinuous forms of his Güell Park, material he also used in his Sagrada Familia, a church begun in the Gothic and continued after the turn of the century in the new style; fantastic lavalike eruptions of forms in the swirling finials and crockets nervously reach for each other in the bustling and animated façade. In 1905-7 the exuviations and undulations of the Batlló and Milá houses add a plasticity that is sculptural rather than architectural.

Others contributed in several ways to the evolution of Art Nouveau: in New York Louis Comfort Tiffany with Favrille glass, and in Paris René Lalique and Emile Gallé with luscent vases elegantly shaped; in Nancy designers Louis Majorelle and Auguste and Antonin Daum; in Germany Otto Eckmann and Hermann Obrist. Gaillard, Plumet, Selmersheim, Vallin, and Riemerschmid are outstanding as furniture designers. Examples of jewelry by Tiffany and Lalique are still highly prized. Art Nouveau set the creative mood for the 1900's, though it soon gave way to the competitive Modern Movement vaunting chaste and restrained forms.

5

THE
NEW CENTURY
1900–1925

Severini: *Blue Train*. 1914.
Solomon R. Guggenheim Museum.

■ What was Europe like in 1900? The mode for living was created in Paris and London, those two great centers of civilization described by Henry James, John Galsworthy and Marcel Proust. A rich and privileged collector at the opening of the century still turned for his latest acquisitions to the great salon, which had absorbed Impressionism into its official style. The Academic styles continued unchecked, with connoisseurs eagerly buying the works of such famous painters as the Dutch Israels and Mauve, or the French Bouguereau and Bonnat, and of other nationals working in an acceptable style. Today these painters are out of fashion (Galsworthy describes their gradual decline), but in their time they were the teachers of many young men who have since become well-known modern masters. The modern vision has left no room for these once great men, though when they are moved from their museum hiding place they frequently offer surprising revelations: once rejected fathers, they are now becoming acceptable grandfathers as their time becomes further removed from us.

The rich patron of 1900 ordered from his architect a building in one of the great national styles of the past: neo-eighteenth century in France, neo-Georgian in England. If possible his furnishings were authentic pieces from the past, and failing this, new ones done in the old spirit. The powerful bourgeoisie cluttered

1. Derain: *Cagnes*. 1910.
Art Institute of Chicago.

2. Picasso: *Family of Saltimbanques*. 1905.
National Gallery of Art, Washington.
(Chester Dale Collection)

up their homes with "traditional" pieces recently
made, overstuffed, overdecorated, and conspicuously
opulent, set off by palms and velvets. Louis Sullivan
foresaw in the Chicago exhibition of 1893 (the Paris
fairs of 1889 and 1900 were not very different) that
the eclectic style of architecture, drawing so heavily
on the past that it stifled new development, was the
taste that would prevail for a long time. He was quite
right: until 1914 the standard building, conceived
along traditional lines and heavily ornamented, was
decorated outside and inside in a kind of Beaux-Arts
or Victorian style drawing on every past fashion,
padded and fringed and suggesting dust in every line.

Against this background appeared a young Spaniard
associated with every episode in the turbulent unfolding of contemporary art. In 1900 academically trained
Pablo Picasso (born in 1881) arrived in Paris. Three
years before, the great Caillebotte Collection had been
offered to the French state and the Impressionists were
about to enter the national collections of the Louvre.
This bequest met with some hostility; a number of
artists were still unacceptable, as was Cézanne. But
young painters were impressed by the achievement of
Cézanne and Seurat, Van Gogh and Gauguin, whose
works were increasingly exhibited. At the same time
the young generation turned to its own set of old
masters (as does every new generation of painters)

for the sources of its new vision. Picasso, impressed
with Lautrec and some of the poster artists, found
inspiration in El Greco. For his Blue and Pink Periods,
Picasso drew freely on the old master's emotional distortions, using at the same time the evocative, simplified outlines and thematic substance derived from the
Symbolists. Starving beggars and melancholy acrobats,
forlorn musicians and derelict women move despair-
ingly through his canvases; the fine emaciation of their
spirit and tragic isolation are described in soft blue and
later rose tones beautifully flattened in their monu-

mental figures.

In the newly organized Salon d'Automne of 1905 appeared paintings by a group who were dubbed the Fauves (Wild Beasts). Matisse, the most outstanding of this group, exhibited with Rouault, Derain, Marquet, Puy, Manguin, Camoin; and the next year Dufy and Braque joined, with Vlaminck, Valtat, and Friesz. Many of the Fauves had come out of the studio of Gustave Moreau, the fin-de-siècle, determinedly decadent and exotic painter. An excellent teacher, he had exploited all the forms and colors then at the disposition of the painter to saturate a given canvas with deliberate fantasies, forced allegories, and personal mythologies, sometimes effective in felicitous compositions and daring color combinations.

The Fauve style was a violent one, deriving from the heightened emotionalism and pure colorism of Van Gogh, the arabesqued forms of Gauguin, the audacious exaggerations of Toulouse-Lautrec, the perspective-negating and simultaneous vision of Cézanne, the color contours in Seurat and other Pointillists. Henri Matisse (1869-1954) used areas of pure color, primaries contrasting with each other, though at times he deliberately chose uncomplementary and arbitrary combinations with startling results. His compositions were contained in large simplified decorative elements moving vigorously over the surface and setting up marked rhythms; in the contours of his figures essentials are stressed and details eliminated except when they reinforce the rhythmic beat of the motif. This system is carried to the extreme—the elements of the painting reduced, but insistent. Maurice de Vlaminck (1876-1958), less intellectual and deliberate than Matisse, used the pure palette of Van Gogh in an explosive way: bright unmixed colors assert his simple themes boldly on his canvas, an "orchestration of pure colors" with emotional fury. Later in his desolate landscapes of World War I this aggressively bright color gave way to vibrant Cézannesque planes describing the scene. In his last years a thick brush emphasized an often recurring theme of nervous houses under a heavy sky. His friend André Derain (1880-1954) shared Vlaminck's interest in Negro and Pre-Columbian sculpture, Gauguin, and Cézanne; but he was more interested in the museum world, archaic, medieval, and quattro-cento art, which freely inspired many of his composi-tions. In time he abandoned the riotous Fauve concepts for clear, figurative, and rounded forms related to real space, conservatively rendered with little or no distor-tion. Albert Marquet (1875-1947), the most cautious of this group, blocked out forms in their silhouettes, suppressing details, simplifying in this way his favorite theme of buildings related to land and water. In con-trast, audacious Raoul Dufy (1877-1953) expounded a joyous theme of human activity on the beach, in the studio, at concerts, at races; his sturdy color areas vibrate restlessly alongside and even across defining lines, which also surge recklessly through the calli-graphic composition. Louis Valtat, in his large decora-tive paintings with superficially bright color enlacing patterned human form, Jean Puy, and Henri Manguin seem closer to an Impressionist idiom sheltering within this style; and Charles Camoin even more so as he worked with Renoir himself. Kees van Dongen soon left the bright Fauve group to paint portraits and figures that have a certain lascivious and satiric bra-vado, while Othon Friesz retained the style in a vigor-ous brushwork to compensate for the eclipsed color. Humanitarian Georges Rouault (1871-1958) adapted this new style to a Daumier tradition as he portrayed the sinister aspects of life: eerie prostitutes, unjust judges, and suffering and desolate mankind, the dark world of his compassion struggling within a Catholic faith. He moves from the congenial medium of blue gouache to thick oil impasto energetically outlined in a rough black resembling the leaded contours of figures in the stained glass that influenced him, a manner most effective in his tragic lithographs.

In 1906 Picasso was introduced to Negro sculpture by his Fauve friends, while Cézanne's geometric vision suggested new paths to him. In 1907 Picasso painted his *Demoiselles d'Avignon,* characterized by a barbaric simplicity in the arrangement of space and the construction of figures. Its savage directness and emotional intensity belong to the trend of Expressionism originating in Van Gogh and exploited by the Fauves and others, yet its passionately abstract construction points elsewhere.

A counteraction and countermovement to Fauvism is Cubism, its emphasis placed on the intellectual and orderly world of the classical tradition, a world to which physicists and mathematicians might relate. Cubism originated in the experiments of Georges Braque (born in 1882) and his friend Picasso. In time poet Apollinaire became the official spokesman for the group and in 1913 wrote its history. In Cubism the painter presents a simultaneous vision of his subject: the spectator is able to consider the object from several angles at once, the object itself being distributed over several planes of the work. The planes are themselves not subject to the laws of real space but marvelously flexible in their ability to lose the parallelism of their volumetric structure; parts reappear in new relations logical only in the context of the work. Since the artist was engrossed with his new found self-constructing space, color became secondary and gravitated to grays and browns.

In Cubism's next phase the sheer form of the object supplied its own motif, and isolated on the canvas it generated curves and lines that flowed out of it; any

Matisse: *Le Luxe.* 1907.
Museum of Modern Art, Paris.
(Arch. Photo)

Rouault: *Self Portrait.*
1926. Lithograph.

necessity of recording the reality that had once inspired them was discarded. The Cubists then began
arranging on their canvases actual fragments of reality
—newspapers or bits of scrap; to these they geared the
fictional world of their picture, constructed to function
as a self-creating entity containing the plane and non-
plane in a decorative whole. In this pasting technique,
called collage, odds and ends of papers were assembled
as partners with each other or with the traditional
paint, or with such nontraditional elements as sand,
veneers, caning, and so on. By isolating concrete fragments in such abstract entities the artist emphasized
the picture's independence of visual reality or senti-

Dufy: *The Flag-Decked Street*. 1906.
Private Collection, Paris. (Arch. Photo)

ment. From this point Cubism could dispense with context and meaning and relation altogether, turn against the real world, and become abstract.

On the eve of World War I others joined the movement, which had entered a decorative phase: Juan Gris (1887-1927) worked with measured surface patterns and broad simplified designs, the construction of his work becoming pellucid and architectonic. Jean Metzinger made of the style a pleasant ornamental pastiche as did Albert Gleizes, who collaborated with him in 1912 on a book about the Cubists. Louis Marcoussis also belonged to this group. Fernand Léger (1881-1955) carried the style into the mid-century; he showed in

Picasso: *Les Demoiselles d'Avignon.* 1907.
Collection of Museum of Modern Art, New York.

his work clear arrangements of solid geometric basic
forms. Simply juxtaposed they become the denominator
for the human figure and its environment, and in time
for the machines, bicycles, and steel skeletons of buildings appearing in his later work. In Cubism, Apollinaire mentions Orphism as the "art of painting the
whole with elements borrowed not from the visible
reality," but from the reality created by the artist.

After such subjects as the *Eiffel Tower,* Robert Delaunay (1885-1941) turned to his *Circular Forms:* "colored themes, without traditional intervention or literary or symbolic explanations," bright geometric circle and rectangles. The Americans Morgan Russell and Stanton Macdonald-Wright worked in this same idiom, calling it Synchronism. The styles derived from Cubism were many; few artists have escaped its strong influence, as *ism* after *ism* followed with great rapidity.

Out of Cubism grows a peculiar flat abstraction where structure is subordinated to surface arrangement. Carrying this tendency to the extreme in order to isolate a pictorial purity, a Russian group, led by Kasimir Malevich (1878-1935) and El Lissitzky (1890-1941), created Suprematism. Malevich and the poet Vladimir Maiakovski collaborated on its manifesto of 1915. For them, form unassociated with objects and reduced to plane geometry functioned with elementary colors as coordinate factors in a binary creation. Constructivism, another Russian movement of this time, included Moholy-Nagy, Tatlin, Rodchenko, Pevsner, and Gabo; in their work form and color are derived from the properties of materials and spun into a three-dimensional creation in which tension, twisting, turning, and finally fusion of contrasting objects explore dynamized space. Here Antoine Pevsner excels in his conceptions of movement within a self-defining object.

Founded in 1917, the De Stijl group of Piet Mondrian (1872-1944) and Theo van Doesburg (1883-1931) showed a preference for the simplest form of rectangle coordinated with the purest color to build up large architectural patterns related to the function of the wall. Proposing forms suitable for modern life,

De Stijl had a great influence on modern architecture, especially on the Bauhaus in Germany. In France Amédée Ozenfant and Le Corbusier advocated Purism: pure and organic forms conceived architecturally and mechanistically were subordinated to their functional context, aesthetic machines to decorate the "machines for living," as their houses were called.

Concurrent with Cubism and drawing heavily on it, yet attacking it at the same time, Italian Futurism was formed in Paris in 1909 and proclaimed in a *Manifesto* the next year. Anarchist and Fascist, the Futurists were an active and short-lived but important group with the poet Marinetti as its prophet. Like Léger they exulted in industrial civilization and drew on it for their inspiration, complaining at the same time that Cubism was static and lacked tension, strength, power, movement—all things that were modern. War represented the apogee of modern life; Nietzsche was their guide. They felt modern forces could be made to function in their work: a famous example is Giacomo Balla's *Dog on Leash*, where the elements of time and motion are introduced by the repetition of human and animal legs. Gino Severini in his *Red Cross Train* of 1914 suggests the creed of the group by using a motley of disparate details in agitated rhythm. Carlo Carrà in *Simultaneity, Woman on a Balcony* remains close to the Cubist technique; while Luigi Russolo's *Lines and Force of the Thunderbolt* is a more convincing example of Futurist aims: writhing wavelike forms are shocked into turbulent motion by repeated lightning flashes attacking the picture's center. The most successful and interesting Futurist was Umberto Boccioni (1882-1916): his *Decomposition of Figures*

1. Braque: *Violin and Palette*. 1910.
Solomon R. Guggenheim Museum.

2. Gris: *Fruit Bowl on Checkered Cloth*. 1917.
Solomon R. Guggenheim Museum.

3. Léger: *Woman in Green and Red*. 1913.
Museum of Modern Art, Paris. (Arch. Photo)

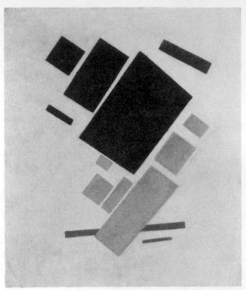

Malevitch: *Suprematist Composition*.
(Airplane Flying). 1914.
Collection Museum of Modern Art, New York.

describes successive states of the human figure in multiple moments of time and in fluid dynamic space,
something he also attempts in his famous sculpture
Unique Forms of Continuity in Space of 1913. Their
mercurial contemporary Giorgio di Chirico in his
own metaphysical school succeeds in grafting the element of time onto his paintings, not a visual but a
visionary time of memory echoing the influence of
Arnold Böcklin: isolated forms cast strange shadows
in a composite sunlight where a dreamlike space re-
cedes forever away from the spectator. Another compatriot, Amedeo Modigliani (1884-1920), worked at
the same period in another style: his large flat figures
reveal taut and simplified arabesques of Negro sculpture; endowed with individual refinement and sub-

Mondrian: *Composition 2*. 1922.
Solomon R. Guggenheim Museum.

tlety, their wistful faces express a remote spiritual suffering.

In Germany other groups were active: in 1905 *Die Brücke* (The Bridge) in Dresden was formed by Ernst Kirchner (1880-1938), Karl Schmidt-Rotluff and Erich Heckel, among others, and joined in the following year by Emil Nolde and Max Pechstein. Inspired by Van Gogh, Munch, and Gauguin they painted in a charged emotional style, emphasizing the brutal and primitive in contemporary civilization. To simplify boldly they used the resources of African art and the frightening tradition of German artists such as Grünewald; barbarism, psychotic unrest, and spiritual distress are conveyed in their works by multiple distortions, unresolved color combinations, and tortured line. Influ-

3

1. Kirchner: *The Street*. 1913.
Collection Museum of Modern Art, New York.

2. Balla: *Dog on Leash*. 1912.
A. Conger Goodyear Collection.

3. Modigliani: *Jacques Lipchitz
and His Wife*. 1916. Art Institute of
Chicago. Helen Birch Bartlett Collection.

enced by their sources too, Oscar Kokoschka (born in 1886) shows a similar vehement brushwork in his emotional portraits and landscapes.

After an abstract Expressionist phase in 1910, Wassily Kandinsky (1866-1944), joined in 1911 by Franz Marc (1890-1916) and later by Paul Klee (1879-1940), formed a group called *Der Blaue Reiter* (The Blue Rider). Their highly personal styles are derived from Fauvism and Cubism, from Negro and post-Impressionist art. Kandinsky disarticulates these earlier styles into spacial and coloristic incoherencies taunting in their emotional turbulence; energetic and elastic space and a curious self-contained dynamic vibration of color areas maintain a high pitch of excitement in his canvases. Contrasting with this wild *con fuoco* is the *andante cantabile* world of Franz Marc in his abstracted and mystical portraits of animals rendered with quiet bright colors and falciform movements. Paul Klee, working intimately on a small scale, reduced his message to witty and philosophic lines and ironic and skeptical hieroglyphs of color motifs echoing children's art and other primitive totemistic representations; their sharp communicability is enhanced by the artist's imaginative titles.

With Klee and Marc Chagall (born in 1887) the art of this time began to show another direction; for both are personal, introspective, and imaginative artists

175

Chagall: *The Yellow Tree.* 1948.
Museum of Modern Art, Paris.
(Arch. Photo)

occupied with interior images where attitudes and
states of mind rephrased by memory retreat from the
dull facts of the visual world. In the compositions of
his landscapes with buildings and figures Chagall owes
much to his French colleagues, to their dislocated cubistic space in which flexible and spiraling movement is
possible; to this he has added a nostalgia of time,
dreams of his childhood's Russian village and recollec-
tions of his Parisian years. Like Klee, Chagall is literary and fantastic, satiric and ironic in an unembittered
and resigned way. Elsewhere in Europe, Cubism ap-

peared in different guises, as in England in the Vorticism of Wyndham Lewis, which after World War I evolved into a conservative style.

Another significant movement was *Neue Sachlichkeit* (New Objectivity) in Germany; Otto Dix and George Grosz returned to a sharp, precise representation of objects bathed in a brisk light. In the postwar twenties these artists while apparently objective, as they claimed to be, distorted reality to point up social despair and a revolutionary political message. In America Charles Sheeler represented this movement in industrial scenes where sheer flat surfaces of wall and roof join the fine cylinders of chimney stacks and tubing, with an effect that is Cubist when not photographic. Max Beckmann (1884-1950) came of age with this style but like Grosz soon turned to distorted Expressionistic scenes of human torment and suffering.

The feverish painting activity in Europe had its reverberation in the United States. Alfred Stieglitz in his New York gallery held small exhibitions of the work of many of the pioneer artists. In 1910 he showed paintings by such European-inspired painters as Marsden Hartley, Arthur Dove, Max Weber, and John Marin. Hartley (1877-1943) revealed a Cubist-Expressionist background in his large tactile forms roughly painted on rude canvases, while Dove (1880-1946) utilized decorative Orphic patterns in rhythmic compositions. Max Weber (1881-   ) was inspired by the evolutions of the French School and Marin (1870-1953) by Cézanne's water-color technique, which he translated into his own vibrant decorative landscapes. Charles Demuth adapted a modified Cubistic vocabulary to his intimate water colors, and Joseph Stella a Cubist-Futurist one

1. Bellows: *Dempsey and Firpo*. 1924. Collection of Whitney Museum of American Art, New York.

2. Sheeler: *Interior*. 1926. Collection of Whitney Museum of American Art, New York.

3. Sloan: *Backyards, Greenwich Village*. 1914. Collection of Whitney Museum of American Art, New York.

in his scenes of New York and its bridges. There are many others, such as Georgia O'Keeffe, with varying personal styles. The most significant event for the art activity of the time was the New York Armory Show of 1913 in which many of these native avant-garde painters exhibited with the Europeans who had inspired them.

This avant-garde movement was isolated from the stream of realism coming from the beginning of the century and represented by the Ash-Can School or The Eight. In protest against the American academic equivalent of the Paris salon, John Sloan (1871-1951), Robert Henri (1865-1929), William Glackens (1870-1938), Everett Shinn (1876-1953), Maurice Prendergast (1859-1924), Arthur B. Davies (1862-1928), George Luks (1867-1933), and Ernest Lawson (1873-1939) joined together in 1908 to exhibit their paintings —done not in the genteel salon manner but in an Impressionist (Prendergast and Lawson), semi-Symbolist

(Davies), or Manet (Sloan, Luks, and Henri) manner, while Glackens absorbed Renoir's style and Shinn, Degas'. George Bellows (1882-1925) joined this group too, and with them painted realist scenes of life in a great city; his vigorous brushwork and color used in an intense personal way are compelling accents in his original compositions; he is much appreciated today along with the bright decorator Prendergast.

By 1900 Rodin had begun to take his place as the foremost sculptor of his day, though others were still awarded the official commissions. At the great exhibition of 1900 he appeared alongside men who were more appreciated by the general public: Falguière, Chapu, Dalou, Frémiet. For the *Gate of Hell* he continued to sculpt details which furnished endless ideas for separate statues in marble and bronze. Among his students Antoine Bourdelle (1861-1929) adapted his doctrines, further heightening the dramatic effect by forceful distortions and surging emotionality as in his war monument of 1893-1902 for the town of Montauban. In time Bourdelle discovered an archaic Greek path. Influenced by the Gothic as well as the classical, the sculptor managed to extract an intensity of feeling from his animated surfaces, as in the heroic statues for his Alvear monument of 1923. His students and admirers were numerous (even Lenin came to listen to him lecture) and his style had an international influ-

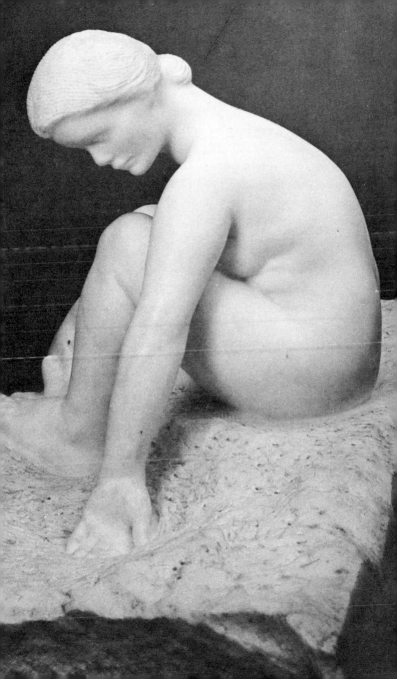

ence. In this humanistic tradition of sculpture are Charles Despiau's finely modeled portrait heads and the work of Charles Malfray.

Rodin's influence continued in another direction: Rumanian Constantin Brancusi (1876-1957) in his early years showed a preference for the Impressionist style of Rodin, blending all the planes of the sculpture into one continuous svelte form; this *sfumato* effect unified the sculptured mass as shadow moved softly in and out over the continuously modulated surface. Ready to absorb Cubism and Futurism, Brancusi took this soft style and ironed the delicate shadows out of it, simplifying further until the essential form alone appeared. In *Bird in Space* of 1919 he refined the form of the object so that even the definition of features need not break the rhythm of the merging parts; he further isolated the upswinging energy inherent in flight in a movement rising subtly away from the axial point. Under the influence of Rodin and Bourdelle, Henri Matisse sculptured his *Slave*, but several years later in his *Reclining Nude* he absorbed their lesson into his own Fauve style with a vigorous compositional arrangement and a strong *contraposto*.

After years of Symbolist painting Aristide Maillol (1861-1944) transferred to sculpture his theme of mythological nude women: in his *Mediterranean* of 1901 he shows his penchant for the tight and simplified forms of archaic Greece, for Aegina rather than Athens. A fine tranquility moves through his work, even when he is concerned with energetic movement as in *Chained Action* and *Desire;* a classical distribution of each segment of the work prevails throughout so that motion is evenly interlocked in an all-over design. Wilhelm Lehmbruck (1881-1919), originally inspired by Maillol, in his *Kneeling Woman* of 1911 added an Expressionist pathos by elongating and refining the figure and emphasizing its sentiment. Encouraged by Maillol, Renoir also produced sculpture, the loose forms of his painting simplified into bronzes and terracottas stroked into warm round shapes. To this period of innovation and discovery belong the sculptures of Amedeo Modigliani. In his *Stone Head* and in similar pieces the derivation from Negro art is apparent, the source metamorphosed by subtle refinement and expressive simplification of form. Jacob Epstein (1880-1959), who knew many of these sculptors and was influenced by their work, excelled in rugged and forceful portraiture. Ernst Barlach (1870-1938) added an intense Gothicism to his Expressionist tortured figures. Most interesting among the experiments in manipulation of space in sculpture was the work of Pablo Picasso. After executing several heads reflecting the fragile melancholy of his blue and rose paintings, he turned to the style of *Head of a Woman* of 1909; cubistically conceived, the face is analyzed into various sharp planes out of which grow auxiliary planes, the hair patterned into architectural braids whose several parts function concomitantly. Energetic shadows accentuate the ridges where the joining planes lead the eye in and out of the turning work. Remarkable too is the Futurist Umberto Boccioni's *Development of a Bottle in Space*, a bronze of 1912, in which the interior and exterior planes of an object simultaneously spiral and interact with each other, the bottle centrifugally peeled into its environment: in "the destruction of the object" there is "no separation of

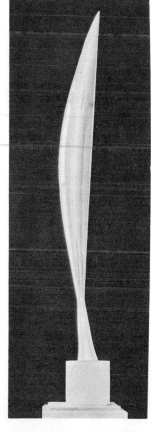

1. Maillol: *Mediterranean*.
1901. Museum of Modern Art,
New York.
(Gift of Stephen S. Clark)

2. Bourdelle: *A Muse*. 1912.
Bourdelle Museum, Paris.

3. Brancusi: *Bird in Space*.
1919. Collection
Museum of Modern Art, New York.

4. Despiau: *Madame Agnes Meyer*.
1929. Private Collection,
Paris. (Arch. Photo)

Picasso: *Head of a Woman.*
1909. Collection
Museum of Modern Art,
New York.

matter and energy." Influenced by Cubism and Futurism, Raymond Duchamp-Villon (1876-1918) produced in 1914 his bronze *Horse,* whose sheer kinetic energy surpasses the nervous shedding motions of Boccioni's bottle. Enfolded by jerky exterior planes and curves, the mechanical thrust of an ostensible drive shaft and gear replaces animal muscular articulation; its movement has the logical intensity of a machine beating out the rhythm of purposeful action. Other sculptors continued the Cubist tradition: Alexander Archipenko constructing with slices of related forms; Henri Laurens (1885-1954) for whom all the faces of the sculpture have an "equal and self-same importance" with polychrome used to eliminate the variations of light; Jacques Lipchitz (born in 1891) involved in placid architectonic sequences of planes in stone, and later in strong rhythmic contortions or savagely imposing totemesque constructions with severe girders of interacting spine punctuated at the summit by two ocular cavities.

In architecture at the turn of the century the United States shared Europe's satisfaction with an eclecticism of past styles: the English and French adaptation of an eighteenth-century vocabulary and the Italian reappraisal of its magnificent Renaissance. With no particular style of its own save the English colonial and the Neoclassical, America borrowed from the styles of history-laden nations and included their Romanesque and Gothic. Architectural inspiration came mainly from the official schools in Paris or London and Rome; traditional forms asserted themselves in the façades, the interiors usually following utilitarian lines, though there the decoration was often opulent. Historical pro-

1. Duchamp-Villon. *Horse*.
1914. Collection Museum
of Modern Art, Paris.
(Arch. Photo)

2. Lipchitz. *Figure*.
1926-30. Sculptor's Collection.

3. Boccioni: *Development
of a Bottle in Space*. 1912.
Collection Museum
of Modern Art, New York.

3

files characterized the civic and commercial buildings
in the great cities: museums and banks adopted the reassuring classical; college and office buildings, the
Gothic. Guided by the prevailing taste, the architectural firm of McKim, Mead and White built in New
York the Vuillard Mansion in 1883-5, the Morgan
Library in 1906. Carrère and Hastings designed and
built the Public Library on Fifth Avenue. In 1908
Goodhue began his West Point buildings in an imaginative castle style. Though steel formed the tall skeleton
of his 1913 Woolworth Building, Cass Gilbert hid the
structure with Gothic ornament. Such historical re-
phrasing continued well into the century. These buildings were permeated with an air of history, didacticism,
traditionalism, and durable eternity; they recalled to
the passer-by his consanguinity with the past.

Opposed to the parade of historical styles of the
Beaux-Arts tradition, groups of architects in several
countries in the early years of our century searched

for a more contemporary idiom. They tended to strip buildings of ornament, excepting whatever derived from structure and materials themselves, and to exploit the newer materials, iron, steel, glass, and reinforced concrete.

Among the early pioneers was Hendrik Berlage (1856-1934) with his 1898 Amsterdam Stock Exchange echoing Richardson's Romanesque style. He stressed the "naked wall in all its sleek beauty"; all structural articulations were sheared to a flat surface. This striking use of unadorned material had appeared elsewhere, as in the Vienna subway's Karlsplatz station by Otto Wagner (1841-1918); his predilection there for slab-like walls was carried over to his Vienna Postal Savings Bank of 1904-6. In this simple interior the emphatic plane surfaces of the walls are sedately set off by the austere curve of the glass roof. This building looks forward to work by Wagner's student Josef Hofmann (1870-1956), who carried this restrained style further in the Purkersdorf convalescent home of 1903-4; and to Adolf Loos (1870-1933) in the 1910 Steiner house in Vienna, where the clarity of horizontal windows set in a stark geometric construction with two boxlike projecting wings seems a variation of the sheer vertical glass rectangles he had used in the interior of his Vienna shop. All such constructions echo Voysey and the English tradition in the eighties and nineties.

1

2

Auguste Perret (1874-1954) in his 1903 Paris apartment houses on the Rue Franklin uses ferro-concrete on a large scale. The façade projects over the entrance, while the concrete skeleton is exposed on the top stories; on the ground floor wide panes of glass between thin supports heighten the light effect; in the interior the flexible ground plan allows varied arrangements of rooms from floor to floor. Comprising several auditoria combined in a single unit, the Théâtre des Champs-Elysées of 1911-4 reveals the new elegance of ferro-concrete; in the foyer the flat decoration stresses the aesthetic potentiality of the new material; balconies are boldly cantilevered into space. Perret and his brother Gustave (1875-1952) continued to explore the possibilities of his preferred medium in the church at La Raincy in 1922-3 and in reconstruction work in Le Havre after World War II.

In 1909 Peter Behrens (1868-1940) constructed his Berlin turbine factory. With contemporary materials like steel and glass shaping the simple and eloquent contour of this huge and dignified building, Behrens created an economical and practical style adaptable to modern industry. Gropius, Mies van der Rohe, and Le Corbusier worked in his studio.

With Walter Gropius (born in 1883) the Behrens clarity of structure is carried further. Glass walls define the cubic volume of the Fagus Factory of 1911 or the appendaged exterior circular staircase of the Cologne model factory in 1914. His most famous building is the Bauhaus at Dessau in 1926. The Bauhaus school and workshop, a fusion of art and industry within an appropriate architectural setting, was formed in Weimar in 1919; many of the leading avant-garde painters and artists participated in its program. Shaped like three arms of a swastika, the bold Bauhaus complex of buildings incorporated schools of designs, studios, dormitories, stages, exhibition rooms, and everything connected with creating and living. Lifted off the ground as though to defy a structural necessity for support, the workshop reveals reinforced concrete floors and vertical supports clearly independent of the continuous glass wall neatly enfolding them. In its structure and free arrangement of rectangular units of varying size the Bauhaus remains the prototype of many later buildings, such as the Lever House and many of its Park Avenue neighbors.

In France a Perret disciple, Le Corbusier (Charles Edouard Jeanneret, born in 1887), championed reinforced concrete building whose clear unadorned exteriors, sliced into volumes, were carried on piers to clarify the relation of weight to support, as in his "Dom-ino" projects of 1915 and his Model House of 1921. Here and in his Citrohan designs of 1918 and his Savoye houses of 1929 he prefers the fine rectangularity of Perret and Behrens. Intellectual in his conceptions, Le Corbusier has the geometrician's delight in long horizontal façade divisions echoing the divisions of the floors. In the free space of the interior the walls can be placed anywhere to vary the shape of the room. He speaks of his buildings as "machines for living" as he stresses their affinity with modern industrial design.

Different from Le Corbusier in architectural temperament, Frank Lloyd Wright (1869-1959), Sullivan's disciple, conceived the house as a complete organism interacting with the plot of ground on which it stood and often constructed with the natural ma-

1

2

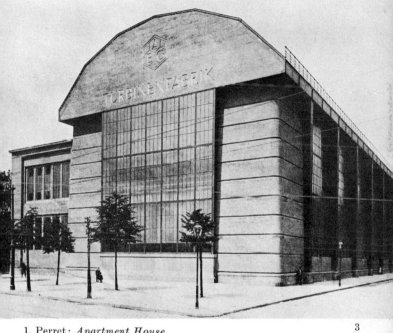

1. Perret: *Apartment House,*
Rue Franklin, Paris. 1902-03. (Chevojon)

2. Gropius: *Bauhaus,*
Lab Workshop, Dessau. 1925-6.
(Photo, Museum of Modern Art, New York)

3. Behrens: *Berlin Turbine Factory.*
1909. (Foto Stoedtner)

3

1. Wright: *Robie House*. 1909.
(Photo, Museum of Modern Art, New York)

2. Rietveld: *Schroeder House, Utrecht*. 1925.
(Foto Stoedtner)

terials of the site. Inessentials are eliminated as the long planes of interiors and exteriors flow easily, one into the other, through cantilevered roofs moving beyond the large windows and porches into overhanging eaves; the planes are often on different levels, as in the Robie House of 1909, each level responding to the rhythm of a separate unit of the house. After 1910 he avoided the flat sites of his ''prairie houses,'' and on the uneven terrain of Taliesin the low-pitched constructions with split-level interiors seem outcroppings of the earth. The Imperial Hotel in Japan, 1915-22, with its concrete piles carried on buried concrete slabs, withstood the earthquake of 1923. Early published books on his architecture helped disseminate his ideas.

Several other architects are admired for projects which, though often confined to the drafting board, remain landmarks in the developing field. Tony Garnier (1869-1948) in his plans for the Industrial City of 1904 indicates ferro-concrete for slabs daringly cantilevered on thin supports and for vigorous cubic houses with sparse decoration. Futurist Antonio Sant'Elia, just before the First World War, drew diagrams of a great city described with powerful élan. Sant'Elia's theme of the dynamic was continued in German Expressionist architecture with Hans Poelzig and Erich Mendelsohn. In Holland Willem Dudok and his associate Jacob Oud contributed to the developing contemporary expression of architecture. Oud and Gerrit Rietveld translated into buildings the flat surfaces and rectangular divisions of the painting and sculpture of the De Stijl group, known also as the Neoplasticists.

Most of the famous examples we know today were clearly defined by 1925.

6
CONTEMPORARY
1925-TODAY

Picasso: *Girl Before the Mirror*. 1932.
Museum of Modern Art, New York.
(Gift of Mrs. Simon Guggenheim)

■ In the second quarter of our century came the last great prototypal art movement—Surrealism, an outgrowth of preceding movements of Dada, Expressionism, Symbolism, and the early Romanticism of artists such as Grandville.

Appearing out of the great crisis of nineteenth century civilization, Dada grew to maturity under the leadership of writer Tristan Tzara in 1916 in Zurich and declined with the war's end. Indifferent to the functions of space and color within a given frame of reference, Dadaists attempted to define not the functioning of aesthetic elements but their nonfunctioning, to express not sense but non-sense. They built up a jarring world of unrelated motifs which shocked by their audacity and delighted by the imaginative juxtaposition of disparate objects, unrelated coefficients making up a startling equation logically at home in its own ironic universe. Such a work is Picabia's *Parade of Lovers,* a functionless mechanism at the service of literary impishness, or the Duchamp brothers' combination of inimical objects to create a new context from an improbable juxtaposition. Motivated by a tantrum of destruction in a self-destructive world, the Dadaists turned against tradition; their ''ready-made'' objects denied their proper functions—a fur-lined teacup, an electric iron with spikes on the bottom—and teased the pragmatic real world into uneasiness.

Like its successor Surrealism, Dada was an exploration in literature and art of man's helplessness to control his world. Dada's accent on destruction and irrationality passed into Surrealism, which sought to re-establish a positive program for art by leaning on the irrational and instinctive and by accepting the ambiguous nature of all things whose meanings were revealed only in the dream or unconscious mind.

Surrealism was announced in 1924 and established the next year with writer André Breton as its head and even today its official apologist. Attacking rationalism, Surrealists emphasized the irrational, the uncontrolled, and accidental, the spontaneous world of thought and action, the subconscious-unconscious, the Freudian, the mystical, the dream-fantasy, the anxiety experienced in the face of dislocation and the ambiguities in everything. The artist does not order the world he depicts; rather he is at the command of the interior impulses (assumed by him to be superior to reasoned action) which direct his creation; and the work once enunciated by that source needs no further explanation. The artist does not understand every symbol in his work, nor does he find it necessary to understand his own creation: what is stated there was intuitively discovered, and intuition has always been Romantically sufficient.

Like Dali some are ready with elaborate explanations on the basis of what they term paranoiac and traumatic experiences, but such explanations do not alter the dream- or trance-like manifesto of the canvas. In Dali's *Persistence of Memory* the world of space and time melting in the heat of the mind is lost in the latitude of subconscious thought, a strange light eating

1. Dali: *Persistence of Memory*. 1931.
Collection Museum of Modern Art, New York.

2. Picabia: *Parade of Lovers*. 1917.
Museum of Modern Art, Paris. (Arch. Photo)

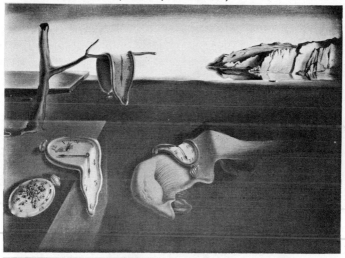

1

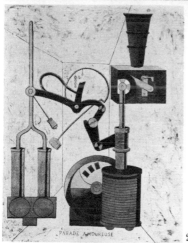

2

Miró: *Landscape*. 1927. Solomon R. Guggenheim Collection.

into the tangible dream world ambiguously presented
as fact, and a dissolving dream reality evoking the
boundary between sleep and consciousness. Max Ernst
emphasized the anguish of the fantastic amorphous, the
shapeless and relentless movement of growth in life
and death; André Masson and Joan Miró played on
the artist's dependence on automatic shapes, used with
a certain irony, which in time become signatures of the
individual artists' idiom. Yves Tanguy preferred the
Dali receding horizon stalked by Miró-like simplified
automatic concretions. Jean Arp, Klee, Man Ray, and
di Chirico belonged to this Surrealist group, as well
as the Belgians Paul Delvaux and Félix Magritte with

their objective canvases charged with literary nostalgia.

This mysterious unconscious is found in the succeeding movement, which is an extension of Surrealism: Neo-Romanticism with Christian Bérard and Eugène Berman, and Pavel Tchelitchew with his trance-like space through which a plunging photographic distortion moves or prenatal transparent children are entwined by the biology of their development.

Many others have moved through this pervasive Surrealist atmosphere. World War I over, Picasso startled his friends with a style that seemed to revert to an Ingres traditionalism. He restored the usual articulation to the figure, stressing the linear outlines and emphasizing the full planal development within the flowing contours. In time he created a sculpturesque monumentality, with overwrought women proclaiming their archaic Greek ancestry or statuesque male flutists in warm marble poses piping Mediterranean tunes.

A decade later the Surrealist concept appears in the overreaching forms of some Picasso figures, in plunging distorted angles of arms and legs straining across dimensionless space, and in representations of bones acting out the drama of flesh or in cruel contortions and dissections of human bodies. In 1937 his preceding styles were synthesized into his great *Guernica:* Surrealist in its vision of cruelty, Cubist in the ordering of the elements that go into it, Futurist in the exposition of a temporal event seen in successive stages, Expressionist in the powerful distortions with which it creates its effects. Thematic and symbolic, it commemorates the Fascist bombing of a Spanish town: the bull of destruction contrasted with the horse-victim of sacrifice; while ruin, death, desolation, and terror, the un-

Picasso: *Guernica*. 1937. Extended loan by the
artist to the Museum of Modern Art, New York.

speakableness beyond picture and word, rise into a
great pyramid contrasted with a chorus of two shriek-
ing women. The paint here is white, gray, and black—
color being banished as it was in Cubism, so that
nothing detracts from the stark message of the work.

The Cubism (or post-Cubism) of Braque during this
time was tempered by an ornamental French classicism,
sharp-featured archaic figures or unassertive still-life
objects arranged in precise areas of subdued color in
compositions always carefully poised. A coarse abrasive

such as sand gives a textural quality to the paint. Like Picasso, he was also active in print-making and book illustration. The production of these two men in this field is considerable, their subjects varying from mythology and fable to Buffon's natural history. Drawn to new media and unusual surfaces, Braque painted on plaster and Picasso explored the field of pottery, setting an example in a great variety of objects for the whole village of craftsmen in Vallauris. Matisse, always a brilliant colorist, painted a number of odalisques against Persian backgrounds, and scenes from balconies along the Côte d'Azur; then he became more abstract and simplified his style to accommodate it to chapel decoration, at Vence in Southern France; afterward, a period of paper cutouts with a majestic Fauve drive added to his reputation as a manipulator of sheer surface space.

Raoul Dufy went on to a new calligraphic style in which scrolling lines moving against bright areas of flat pigment are coordinated with the color though they do not contain it; in this style a large mural represents

Matisse: *Paper Cut-outs, The Esquimau and Other Subjects.* Collection Pierre Matisse.

the history of electricity, a traditional subject with historical figures. Vlaminck and Derain worked through this period, the one in thick impasto paint and dramatic perspective and the other in a cautious conservative style. Chagall continued to explore his \own fantastic folklore in imaginative settings, while Rouault, becoming somber and morally didactic, enlarged on individual pathos and universal tragedy. There are other painters who have contributed to what is loosely known as the School of Paris: Chaim Soutine working in a frenzied Expressionist style that often

L'esquiman

H. Matisse

Dunoyer de Segonzac: *The Meaux Road.*
1932. Museum of Modern Art,
Paris. (Arch. Photo)

borders on rhythmical mania, the subject swept into
the painterly stream of the brush; and Jules Pascin
describing in thin transparent colors the lascivious
leisure of forlorn women.

Others followed a different path, carrying a more or
less traditional style of figure painting into the twentieth century. André Dunoyer de Segonzac is outstanding for his scenes of afternoons on the beach or picnics
in the country done with simplified palette in thick
quiet colors. His friends Legueult and Cavaillès prefer
similar scenes in bright colors. Gernez and Laprade
might fit into such a group. Conservative and advanced
painters decorated the Palais de Chaillot built for the
Paris fair of 1937: Raoul Dufy, Bonnard, Friesz,
Brianchon, Oudot, Waroquier, Dufresne, Planson,

Chapelain-Midy, Souverbie, Marchand, and others. Respect for the human figure and appreciation of traditional pictorial space characterize most of the work there. Many of these Trocadéro painters, admired by the French bourgeoisie, represent a current of French art that continues to produce and wait for its vindication. Alongside these professionals, the naive painter stubbornly pursues his particular vision with a sharp and detailed directness or an unguarded poetic insouciance: Maurice Utrillo and Alphonse Quizet in evocations of Montmartre, Louis Vivin, Camille Bombois, Jean Eve, and Jules Lefranc in simple everyday scenes; or Louis Séraphine and André Bauchant ambitiously interpreting their imaginative world.

In the United States during the thirties, Realism reappeared in the guise of Social Realism, the artist infusing his theme with the mood of discontent by exaggerating what best suited his purpose. The style also suited the aims of Soviet artists because it exalted subject matter, simplified to enhance the impact of its message. In the United States it was popular among a generation of artists awarded commissions by the Works Progress Administration to decorate post offices and other public buildings. Many of today's well-known artists began under the aegis of the WPA and Social Realism. In time the style was tempered with a strain of conservative Expressionism. Examples are Philip Evergood in tenement scenes of suffering children and despairing mothers, Jack Levine in caustic political near-caricatures of brutal wielders of power, Ben Shahn in exciting themes dealing with ordinary activities of lively flat figures with linear features and crumpled shadows. William Gropper and others should be recalled here too.

A branch of this kind of realism may be seen in certain types of regional painting: Thomas Hart Benton in Western farm scenes, Grant Wood in wooden American history of rural places, John Steuart Curry in storms over Texas, Reginald Marsh in raucous descriptions of New York life, and many other artists who stress the picturesque rather than the socially meaningful. Edward Hopper is still admired for his evocative city scenes: under the forlorn light of a late-night café or in faceless alleys and deserted gas stations a nostalgic loneliness envelops apathetic human accidentals. Akin is Charles Burchfield with his haunted Halloween houses. The native scene appears naively in such primitives as John Kane, Louis Eilshemius, grandmothers painting in their leisure time, and many Sunday painters. There continues of course a traditional activity in all kinds of landscape painting; Andrew Wyeth skillfully depicts shore and farm, and there are other solid painters at work elsewhere. Considerately reporting our features are fine portraitists such as Charles W. Hawthorne, or the numerous artists working for Portraits Inc. who carry on the old tradition for patrons with commissions to give.

Mexico had its era of revolutionary social consciousness out of which sprang some excellent artists: historical muralist Diego Rivera (1886-1957), politically militant José Clemente Orozco (1883-1949), social-Surrealist David Siqueiros, and Picassoesque Rufino Tamayo.

In Europe and America a new generation of artists has emerged from the recent world war; their styles are individual, though often they can be identified with particular movements. In France the young Bernard Buffet has been admired for his desolate scenes of humanity with gaunt faces and dazed eyes, angular and skeleton-thin figures moving in an impoverished and depleted world rendered in thorny grays and blacks. Jean Dubuffet is quite different. His style has been called Brute Art: brutalized Paul Klee figures and totemic images are disintegrated with violence into simple, inarticulate, and somber forms, which somehow retain all the memory of their humanity. In disengaged figures performing in disinterested space, he manages to convey his witty message with satiric force and ironic detachment. Abstraction continues with its leading spokesman Alfred Manessier and his follower Jean Le Moal using elongated flowing floral forms in bright colors; or with the Spartan directness of Pierre Soulages' puissant strokes in controlled and reduced space, a method contrasting with the impetuous calligraphy of Georges Mathieu whose impulsive élan spills into nervous, pertinent scribbling. Nicolaes de Staël infused into his abstract themes a vibrant sensibility, while Wolfgang Wols reduced the Surrealist theme to its abstract nerves and fibers, disembodied motifs moving mysteriously through his intimate water colors.

In recent years the balance of painting has tilted temporarily toward abstraction. In America, European abstractionist Hans Hofmann lures onto the siren canvas surfaces his brilliant themes of vigorous color relationship athwart a charged space. Many of the younger generation have watched, admired, and also studied with him.

In the 1950's many artists in New York who had

been active in the forties appeared to cohere into a "school." Known as Abstract Expressionists or Action Painters, these young artists, influenced by the émigré deans of painting and by collectors and dealers from abroad, were inspired by several sources: the emotional turbulence of the Fauves and Kandinsky, from whom they derive their drive, their free-moving forms, the electric charge of the inspiration and the use of wiry or thick thunderbolts, rondels, and rectangles in rivers of flowing and propelled color. Attractive for them too were Miró's capricious amoeba forms and the scribbling caustic ones of Klee, the free penmanship of Masson, and the decorative devices of post-Cubism: in short, forms unattached to any concrete image. This spectacular vocabulary absorbed, the artist learned a new way to paint: the Surrealist had taught him automatic writing; filled with an unconscious desire, an artist long trained in the labyrinths of his craft need only follow his instinct and the resultant combination of color and line could produce an authentic painting; the very action of painting created a work of art.

The new group felt that brush and palette were an unnecessary restraint on the act of painting. Though the old master Hans Hofmann painted with great violence, spattering the paint onto the canvas and delighting in the great flexibility of his energetic forms, Jackson Pollock went further. With large canvases, cheap house paints, and ordinary paint brushes the artist was free of the brain-moving-arm restriction. After attacking his canvas vertically, Pollock now turned it flat on the floor; using not only his hand but his whole body, he applied his paint as he moved over the canvas. In this way he could construct the decora-

1. Shahn: *Handball*. 1939.
Collection Museum
of Modern Art, New York.

2. Hopper. *Nighthawks*. 1942.
Art Institute of Chicago.
(Friends of American Art Collection)

1. Orozco: *Dive Bomber and Tank*. 1940.
Collection of Museum of Modern Art, New York.

2. Buffet: *Pietà*. 1946.
Museum of Modern Art, Paris. (Arch. Photo)

tive scheme as in a dance, dripping and splashing the paint in rhythmic patterns, building each element out of the preceding, though he was never sure what his scheme was to be—rather it suggested itself to him as he worked along. His canvases have the bravura of strong rhythmic qualities, raw textures and patterns in architectonic ribs; later, skeins of color challenge the traditional processes of creating. But he brought his art to a cul-de-sac out of which neither he nor painting could emerge.

Among his colleagues in this "school" are Mark Tobey using calligraphied indications threading their way through a highly charged and complicated surface, Willem de Kooning with his virulent brush and melodramatic themes in which Klee-Dubuffet personages insinuate themselves, Philip Guston entranced with spotted color interplay, Adolph Gottlieb moving from totem-image to later tension-twists, Franz Kline extracting lyrical movement from the bare energy of his black-thrusting spacial drives, and Fritz Bultman in his monumental ordering of space in which movement is mysteriously propelled by some fine emotional energy to describe a painterly equilibrium where mass and force meet.

In the tradition of Miró and Masson are William Baziotes and Theodoros Stamos, their pliant marine structures describing ovular metamorphoses in subtle colors; Matta with translucent fingerforms in fantastic interplay and lewdly energetic movements in cosmic space, Winifred Lam with a more terrestrial universe motivated by long Picassoesque rectangularities, and Graham Sutherland with unique spikey forms. Others prefer a more precise world and vaunt the influences

Dubuffet: *Le Président*. 1945.
Collection Pierre Matisse.

of De Stijl and Constructivism: Josef Albers or Rice-Pereira in a parallelepiped of lines and bands moving through overlapping transparent slabs; Giorgio Cavallon in decorative geometric space, Mark Rothko contrasting shimmering rectangular color areas with counterpart areas striving for monumental integrity. Clifford Still shares this tendency toward special containment in his free forms flowing nervously in positive colors. Stuart Davis continues to add to the post-Cubist decorative tradition with simplified angular forms in bright and easy colors. Robert Rauschenberg is effective as a neo-Dadist singing the high rate of speed with which our civilization creates the debris remaining to haunt us, as is Jasper Johns with more precise contemplative objects. Alberto Burri too concerns himself with this scratched vision as he contrasts the eloquent abrasive surfaces of canvas taut in their humble juxtaposition of worn and allied patches, as does Leon Golub in brute figures majestic and assertive in their desquamated amplitude.

Another tendency in painting is called Magic Realism, an ally of Realism and Surrealism; it investigates the overtones of real appearances, of intransigent objects thrusting athwart a material world of New Objectivity and the photograph, and affixes mystery to the ordinary outside of daily life. Bernard Perlin's world is suffused with a poetic anxiety, Robert Vickrey's with a ritual and orgiastic mood, and Paul Cadmus's and George Tucker's with a caustic disillusionment. Ivan Le Lorrain Albright and Edwin Dickenson pass through the thin boundary of reality, as does Francis Bacon in a macabre vision. Clearly Surrealist are Peter Blume and Kurt Seligmann, while Morris Graves gives

1. Soulages: *Painting.*
1953. Solomon R.
Guggenheim Collection.

2. Hofmann: *Magenta
and Blue.* 1950.
Collection of
Whitney Museum of
American Art, New York.

1

metaphysical overtones to his bird images set in a
whimsical oriental world. Linked with these men,
Joseph Cornell sums up the meaningful in both painting and sculpture with a universe of charged boxes—
sculptural cut-outs in pictorial confrontations.

Sculpture in this generation continues to thrive in the
hands of the old masters. Brancusi developed the vertical and dynamic élan of his *Bird in Space* into the
simplified horizontal form of *The Fish* moving finwise
on a special base so that we can admire its slablike dis-
placement as it solemnly turns; in direct wood carving
such as *Adam and Eve* stark and abstract forms derived from African sculpture symbolically enact their
story. While he preserves the rough texture of some
materials, he gives to others a high finish, always reduc-
ing volumes to their perfect form.

In his search for the essence of natural forms John

2

Flannagan scratchily shaped from a worn granite
boulder his *Triumph of the Egg*. Jean Arp's *Two
Heads* of 1929 is a painted wood relief in which three
kidney curves react against two placid circular shapes.
Henry Moore's *Two Forms* of 1934 echoes in the round
the juxtaposition of such shapes and emphasizes the
tension between the disparate sizes. In *Reclining
Figure* of 1938 Moore cuts through the traditional
solids of sculpture to lead the eye through as well as
over the work, the eye's pleasure in the surface heightened by his emphasis on the ornamental quality of
striations in wood or marble. Barbara Hepworth too
explores tensions and oppositions in contrasting materials. Jacques Lipchitz persists in his complex and
rugged forms with his *Prayer* of 1943, its coarse-sur-
faced bronze wrought into intricate movements suggesting allegorical ritual; while in his *Sacrifice* of five

years later these same allegorical forms are reduced to
severe essentials and broad planes moving starkly
around its violent core. Direct carvers José de Creeft
and William Zorach emphasize the natural textures
of marble and varied stones or wood in their explicit
and normative figures.

Among the contemporary masters Alberto Giacometti
returns to a thin twelfth-century Gothic tradition of
figures depleted by their absorption into the vertical,
while the spirit of isolation withers the physical being
out of the real world. In his use of rope-thin forms
Giacometti negates the solid classical world, while he
diagrams man by grandiose gestures. Germaine Richier
moves along similar paths, though hers is a more brutalized form, shaped by rough bark texture stressing
material and violent movement. Reg Butler conveys
the ascetic tendencies in a more abstract and surrealist
manner.

Constructivists Antoine Pevsner and Naum Gabo produced piquant sculptural machines creating plano-con-
cave and -convex interrelations. In Gabo's case the drafting board supplied the aesthetics of pulsing parabolas
describing special revolutions activated by tangential
motion. His translucent surfaces draw light and shadow into fragilely defined forms over which the eye
slides and shifts, the vision cut or directed by tense
fans of string or metal wire. Pevsner, less clear in his

work, uses cubic forms restlessly scooped out to suggest the intricacies of volume reacting to inner propulsion and outer receptivity. To the De Stijl tradition belong Ben Nicholson's reliefs, clear, geometrically arranged rectangles in simple colors, plane rising thinly over plane in subtle and unassuming laminae. Adding engineering to this tradition, Alexander Calder constructs his pendant Miró shapes in blacks, bright blues, and reds; moved by the wind and creating surprising and ingenuous patterns in the slowly shifting juxtapositions of their different parts, they swim leisurely on their magical axes and flirt with the surrounding space.

In Italy a number of sculptors carry on the old traditions in a new and appealing way; Marino Marini recaptures the sensitive yet vigorous surfaces of the Renaissance in his *Dancer* of 1949, while in the same year his bronze *Horse and Rider* displays all the simplified drives of a naif; his portrait of Stravinsky shows how compelling a work can be realized with economical means. Giacomo Manzù in his *Cardinal* and *Deposition* of 1949 works in a moving Donatelloesque fashion, the forms flattened to heighten the pictorial quality of his sparse scene; though in his statues of cope-clad ecclesiastics he expands his theme to impressive monumentality, always animating his simple surfaces with subtle modulations reflecting an atmospheric envelope. Emilio Greco's nudes and portraits of women

1

2

Burri: *Composition*. 1953.
Solomon R. Guggenheim Collection.

are in this svelte Italian tradition with its careful attention to clear volumetric construction and well-defined themes, though they have an individual overtone of Leonardoesque decadence.

During this time Picasso continued experimenting with sculpture. In a dramatic Rodinesque tradition his *Shepherd Holding a Lamb,* an austere and hieratic bronze of 1944, resumes the allegorical theme of the Good Shepherd as a harbinger of peace at the war's end. In the bronze goat and owls of the fifties there is another tendency at work: collecting all kinds of *objets trouvés* (found or ready-made objects) of a special sort —bolts, nuts, scraps of iron, and various strewn metal pieces of the wrecker's yard—Picasso patched together plaster models from which he made bronze casts. In

these works the texture is coarse and even crude, the surface corroded by details rudely incorporated into his scheme. He often prefers to dissociate parts from their context by dislocating the profiles of the joints and denying them a functional articulation within the figure. The result is something vigorous and painstakingly humble, the humility of common, ordinary, even useless objects now resurrected by their translation into sculpture.

Such rudely archaic forms add to our experience of sculpture by giving a new textured quality that, far from defining the form-enclosing surface, draws impulses from within its porous space-crawling conjugations. Such a work is Theodore Roszak's *Kitty Hawk* of 1947: ruthless conifer shapes of welded and ham-

1. Moore: *Reclining Form*. 1938.
Tate Gallery, London.
(Arch. Photo)

2. Arp: *Two Heads*. 1929.
Collection Museum of Modern Art,
New York.

3. Giacometti:
Man Pointing. 1947.
Collection Museum of
Modern Art, New York.
(Gift of Mrs. John D.
Rockefeller, 3rd)

4. Zorach: *Pegasus*.
1925. Collection
of Whitney Museum of
American Art, New York. (Gift
of Mrs. Juliana Force)

3

4

1. Gabo: *Column*. 1923. Solomon R. Guggenheim Collection.

2. Nicholson: *Relief*. 1939. Collection Museum of Modern Art, New York. (Gift of H. S. Ede)

mered steel, bronze and brass agglomerates in prickly forms through which the eye darts for "blunt reminders of primordial strife and struggle, reminiscent of . . . brute force." Herbert Ferber and David Smith tend to use more concise and clearer abstract forms to evoke their themes, and Louise Nevelson conceives the world in terms of combinable pieces of wood worked into pigeonholed forms, and Richard Lippold in terms of the chaste formulism of his linear compounds. The use of found objects is popular with sculptors: César collects his in the automobile junkyards and cuts and combines them into surprising and interesting shapes which retain their original texture, and through their old function and new employment merge the fanciful with the abstract.

By their pioneer achievement and incessant creativity two old masters dominate the field of contemporary architecture: Frank Lloyd Wright and Le Corbusier. Wright stresses his rapport with nature in work that has overtones of nineteenth-century individualism. In 1936-7 his Falling Water House at Bear Run was planned around an uneven terrain, with parts of the structure audaciously cantilevered over a natural stream and other parts impulsively opened onto the surrounding woods. The 1936-9 Johnson Wax Administration Building emphasizes unexpected forms with striking effect, such as Cretan-like columns mushrooming at the top and tapering at the bottom. Other innovations appear in the 1948 Morris Shop in San Francisco, with its spiral ramp swooping upward beneath a ceiling of contrasting glass disks. The ramp is exploited to its fullest extent in the Guggenheim Museum, its impressive cantilevered spiral sculptured

1

2

1. Roszak: *Spectre of Kitty Hawk*.
1946-7. Collection Museum of
Modern Art, New York.

2. Picasso: *Shepherd Holding
a Lamb*. 1944. Philadelphia
Museum of Art.

3. Manzù: *Cardinal*.
1949. Private Collection.
(Arch. Photo)

3

Wright: *"Falling Water" House*, Bear Run, Pa.
1936-7. (Photo Museum of Modern Art)

out of poured and sprayed concrete, while the scooped-out center funnels to a glass dome.

Unlike Wright, Le Corbusier shows little Romantic identification with nature. In his 1931-2 Swiss Hostel in the Cité Universitaire in Paris he considered the building's relation to its surroundings as he strengthened the piers into great pylons, varied the opaque and transparent glass of the windows in the sun-facing facade, and dramatized the natural state of unfaced concrete, stone, and glass in different units of the building. Above the pylons he revealed the bottom of the building. After commissions in Moscow and Rio de Janeiro and elsewhere he turned to his great work, the Unité d'Habitation in Marseilles in 1946-52, a complex providing for the entire existence of an average community. Here he continued his system of delineated cubic forms of raw-textured concrete cohering in a mass form, carried by great pylons and accented by shallow balconies with color relief. Recently in two extraordinary buildings, strange but sculpturally pleasing, he asserted his mastery as an innovator: in the convent of Sainte-Marie de la Tourette, near Lyons, massive rectangular striations and flat piers open the building to the exterior site; and in Notre-Dame-du-Haut at Ronchamp (almost the opposite in spirit as it withdraws into the interior) the solid surface is broken by rectangles pulsating Mondrian-like with each other; swooping walls are brushed by a cantilevered roof similar to a nun's winged cornet.

Another important figure today is Ludwig Mies van der Rohe. At the Barcelona Exhibition in 1929 influences from Neoplasticism, Le Corbusier, and Gropius were absorbed into his German Pavilion of steel, glass, marble, and travertine, the sweep of its rectangular slab wall contrasting with echoing units. In his Chicago apartment houses of the fifties the Miesian idiom clearly appears in the steel frame sheathed in thin vertical mullions, rectangular spandrels, and tinted glass—a theme continued in his and Philip Johnson's 1956-8 Seagram Building on Park Avenue in New York City; a new spatial extension occurs in the electric glow defining the vespertine quality of volume as it

Le Corbusier:
Unité d'Habitation. Marseilles.
1946-52. (Kidder Smith Photo)

stares from the patterned openings of the black façade
onto its surrounding piazza.

With constant imitation of examples by Mies and
Gropius, a ubiquitous style is rapidly becoming the
common denominator of architecture in the great
cities.

Impressed with the achievements of Mies, Gordon
Bunshaft designed in New York the Park Avenue
Lever House with its glass curtain of tinted green, the
columns, transoms, and mullions enveloped in stainless

Le Corbusier:
Notre-Dame-du-Haut, Ronchamp. 1950-54.
(Kidder Smith Photo)

steel; and on Fifth Avenue the Manufacturers Trust
Company, a transparent panorama of a big bank, the
interior luminously alive and flowing past few visible
supports into the street. Edward Stone works in a different vein; in New York—in the 1937-9 Museum of
Modern Art the horizontal sweep of planes is asserted;
in the same city his own house and the Huntington
Hartford Museum are monolithic dolmens pierced by
regular and rhythmic pores rising impressively to a
defined roof.

235

1. Mies van de Rohe and
P. Johnson: *Seagram Building*.
New York. 1956-58.
2. Bunshaft with Skidmore,
Owings & Merrill: *Lever House*.
New York. 1952.

Many of the foremost European masters came to
America to continue their work. Gropius taught at
Harvard from 1937 to 1953 and later founded The
Architects' Collaborative, a group striving for Total
Architecture or the "reunification of art and science";
from this collective effort are the United States Em-
bassy in Athens, a steel frame with canopied eaves to
shade the glass curtain walls; and, with Pietro Belluschi, the octagonal Pan Am building mushrooming
out of New York's Grand Central Station. Once associated with Gropius, Marcel Breuer later developed
the split-level Butterfly House with sloping roof.
Richard Neutra, influenced by Loos and later by
Wright, continued in the rectilinear style, as in the

1927 Lovell house and his own house in Los Angeles in 1932.

In Europe, present-day architects accomplish an impressive task. In France concrete plays an important role in the new buildings: in Guillaume Gillet's sharp-angled church of Notre-Dame at Royan and in the Saint-Pius X Basilica at Lourdes by Vigo and Freyssinet, the wide parabolic sweep describing the spacious interior is reminiscent of the latter's memorable 1916 dirigible hangar at Orly. In one of the important recent buildings, the Exhibition Hall outside Paris, architects J. de Mailly, B. Zehrfuss, and R. Camelot envisaged a huge turtleback shell growing out of three great piers; jutting from the shell are rectangular units built on

pagoda-like piers; alternating opaque and transparent glass windows are "hung" on the façade. By Zehrfuss, Breuer, and Nervi is the Y-shaped UNESCO building, an essay in concrete, pylons, and glass framed in a grass lawn.

In Italy the theatrical Fascist monumental architecture of the prewar period has been replaced by lively variations of the international style. Chief among the present-day builders is engineer Pierluigi Nervi, who with architects Piacentini and Vitellozzi designed two precast concrete stadia for the 1960 Olympics in Rome; the unusual domes of both edifices contain intricate and

De Mailly, Zehrfuss and Camelot:
C.N.I.T. Exhibition Hall. Outside Paris.

dynamic patterns in concrete. In prefabricated concrete the exposition hall in Turin shows Nervi's skill in clear structural patterns enlivening the soaring interior. Nearby, Riccardo Morandi's Automobile Pavilion carries prestressed concrete beams on inclined columns to emphasize the dynamic functions of weight and support. New work is evident everywhere in Italy.

Postwar England has produced some fine buildings: the Royal Festival Hall of 1951 by Matthew and Martin, industrial buildings by Farmer and Dark, the Nuclear Power Station and Harlow New Town by Gibbard, and Coventry Cathedral by Basil Spence.

1. Spence:
New Cathedral. Coventry.
2. Nervi, Piacentini and
Vitellozzi:
Palazzetto dello Sport. Rome.
1960. (Photo "ENIT")

The Scandinavian countries have produced several outstanding architects. Sweden's Sven Markelius and others considered all the problems of a thriving suburbia in the town-section of Vällingby in Stockholm; in the same city Gunmar Asplund provided an impressive and dignified crematorium. Finland produced Eliel Saarinen and his son Eero; and Alvar Aalto, famous for his Turun Sanomat Plant of 1930 in Turku and the nearby tuberculosis sanatorium at Paimio in 1933. Aalto designs the furniture and fixtures for the interiors, as in the Tautatalo office building in Helsinki. His 1939 Unila Plant near Kotka employs a cubic concentration of buildings well adapted to the rugged site and within walking distance of a nearby village he also planned. In Denmark Arne Jacksen's S.A.A. headquarters and Town Hall rise in a Miesian architectural idiom.

Many architects are daring and experimental. Eero Saarinen, once apprentice to his famous father, designer of the Cranbrook School in Michigan, worked in a Miesian straight-edged style in the General Motors Technical Center in Michigan and a curvilinear one in the Kresge Auditorium of the Massachusetts Institute of Technology. In his TWA terminal at Idlewild Airport the roof is composed of four great concrete shells resting on huge supports; two violin-shaped claws extend to embarcation points. The sculptural mobility of the whole design and the elasticity of parts articulating out of each other look back to the work of others: to Constructivist Berthold Lubetkin in his 1933 London Penguin Pool, and to Wright's recent Guggenheim Museum, the plans of which were well known for more than a decade. The importance of such buildings

Fuller: *Geodesics Dome.*
St. Louis.

lies in their sculptural flexibility to turn in every conceivable direction, and architect John Johansen shows how original the plan can become in the Schwarzenback house in Connecticut. Others contribute something different. Charles Eames uses prefabricated elements to construct his curt houses with Mondrian regularity; he also applies his new techniques to scooped-out, body-fitting plywood furniture. Robert Maillart has redefined the parabolic leap of concrete bridges through space. Oscar Niemeyer in his plans for Brasília assembles his forms with ingenuity, as does Eduardo Torroja in his Spanish buildings and Felix Gandela in his Mexican ones. R. Buckminster Fuller considers the

Saarinen: *New TWA Terminal.*
Kennedy International Airport, New York.

mass production of homes, shelters, and industrial interiors economically constructed from his geodesic domes based on four- and eight-sided figures.

With such architectural activity new problems of urban planning arise. In New York City the planning of complex centers integrates the styles of many distinguished architects into one homogeneous unit: in New York, Rockefeller Center's Reinhard and Hofmeister; Corbett, Harrison and MacMurray; Hood and Fouilhoux; and Lincoln Center's Johnson, Harrison, Abramowitz, Saarinen, Bunshaft, and Belluschi—all famous men who have left the imprint of their ideas on today's cities.

The contemporary architect is increasingly aware of the necessity for collaborating with the painter and sculptor in evolving his complex structures. European designers feel the necessity for an integrated architectural statement in which all the arts have a role, as in the Paris UNESCO Building with murals by Picasso and sculpture by Moore. Painters and sculptors cooperate in the elaboration of Rockefeller Center. In Lincoln Center sculpture now participates in defining the interiors, as Richard Lippold's tentacular work for the Grand Foyer of the Philharmonic Hall. Sculpture inside and outside such monumental buildings, and mural painting—now developed to a point where its expansive areas are adaptable for such functions—will become adjuncts of architectural exploration and community experience.

With his companion creator in the other arts, the architect of our century exults in new forms. Like the painter and sculptor he thinks in terms of huge constructions as he responds to the grandiose schemes of the expanding industrial civilization. To fill the new interiors, the designer in all fields attempts to parallel the animating spirit of contemporary creation. In general, like the architect, the designer prefers the fine straight edge of forms juxtaposable and capable of re-arrangement; he also explores the forms found in nature and exploits the round and curving and often the fantastic. In the main, shapes are simple and restrained and reduced to essentials, because the designer has absorbed this concept of our time. And every creator in the arts feels the need to create within the realm of a time-spirit that guides his mind and hand as it guided his predecessors in all human activity.

SELECTED BIBLIOGRAPHY

GENERAL: A. H. Barr Jr., *Masters of Modern Art*, New York, 1954 / M. Brion, *Romantic Art*, New York, Toronto, London, 1960 / M. W. Chamberlain, *Guide to Art Reference Books*, New York, 1959 / H. Focillon, *La peinture au XIXe siècle*, Paris, 1927 / H. Gardner, *Art through the Ages*, New York, 1959 / S. Giedion, *Space, Time and Architecture*, Harvard, 1954 / R. Goldwater, *Primitivism in Modern Painting*, New York, 1938 / A. Hauser, *The Social History of Art*, New York, 1951, 1958 / R. Huyghe (ed.), *L'Art et l'homme*, Vol. 3, Paris, 1961 / H. R. Hitchcock, *Architecture 19th and 20th Centuries*, Baltimore, 1958 / H. W. & D. Janson, *Picture History of Painting*, New York, 1962 / C. Jones, *Architecture, Today and Tomorrow*, New York, 1961 / A. Malraux, *Voices of Silence*, Paris, 1952; New York, 1953 / A. Michel (ed.), *Histoire de l'art*, Vol. 8, Paris, 1925 / R. Motherwell (ed.), *Dada Painters and Poets*, New York, 1951 / B. S. Myers, *Modern Art in the Making*, New York, 1959 / N. Pevsner, *Pioneers of Modern Design*, New York, 1949 / N. Pevsner, *Outline of European Architecture*, Baltimore, 1960 / P. Pollock, *The Picture History of Photography*, New York, 1958 / M. Praz, *The Romantic Agony*, London, 1933; New York, 1956 / E. P. Richardson, *Way of Western Art: 1776-1914*, Harvard, 1939 / R. Rosenblum, *Cubism and Twentieth Century Art*, New York, 1960 / G. E. Kidder Smith, *New Architecture of Europe*, New York, 1961.

UNITED STATES: J. I. H. Baur, *American Painting in the Nineteenth Century*, New York, 1953 / M. W. Brown, *American Painting from the Armory Show to the Depression*, Princeton, 1955 / T. Hamlin, *Greek Revival Architecture in America*, New York, 1944 / J. T. Flexner, *Pocket History of American Painting*, New York, 1957 / S. Hunter, *Modern American Painting and Sculpture*, New York, 1959 / O. W. Larkin, *Art and Life in America*, New York, 1949, 1960 / I. McCallum, *Architecture U.S.A.*, London, 1959 / L. Mumford, *Roots of Contemporary American Architecture*, New York, 1952 / E. P. Richardson, *American Romantic Painting*, New York, 1944 / J. T. Soby, *Younger American Painters*, New York, 1954 / T. E. Tallmadge, *Story of Architecture in America*, New York, 1936.

LATIN AMERICA and CANADA: D. W. Buchanan, *Canadian Painters*, London, 1945 / P. M. Bardi, *The Arts in Brazil*, Milan, 1956 / J. Gómez, *Cuban Painting of Today*, Havana, 1944 / H. R. Hitchcock, *Latin-American Architecture since 1945*, New York, 1955 / L. Kirstein, *The Latin-American Collection of the Museum of Modern Art*, New York, 1943 / H. Mindlin, *Modern Architecture in Brazil*, New York, 1956 / B. S. Myers, *Mexican Painting in Our Time*, New York, 1956.

BRITAIN: T. S. R. Boase, *English Art, 1800-1870*, Oxford, 1959 / K. Clark, *The Gothic Revival*, London, 1928, 1950 / R. Fry, *Reflections on British Painting*, New York, 1934 / H. R. Hitchcock, *Modern Architecture in England*, New York, 1937 / R. Ironside, *Pre-Raphaelite Painters*, London, 1948 / F. D. Klingender, *Art and the Industrial Revolution*, London, 1947 / I. McCallum, *Pocket Guide to Modern Buildings in London*, London, 1951 / N. Pevsner, *The Buildings of England, Vol. 1: London*, London, 1947 / D. Pilcher, *The Regency Style, 1800-1830*, London, 1947 / H. Read, *Contemporary British Art*, Harmondsworth, 1961 / R. &

S. A. Redgrave, *A Century of British Painters*, London, 1947 / A. C. Ritchie, *Masters of British Painting 1800-1950*, New York, 1956 / J. K. M. Rothenstein, *Introduction to English Painting*, London, 1933 / R. Turnor, *Nineteenth Century Architecture in Britain*, London, 1950 / R. H. Wilenski, *English Painting*, Boston and New York, 1956.

FRANCE: B. Dorival, *La peinture française*, Paris, 1946 / B. Dorival, *Twentieth Century Painters*, New York, 1958 / W. Friedlaender, *From David to Delacroix*, Harvard, 1952 / L. Hautecoeur, *Histoire de l'architecture*, Paris, 1952-57 / L. Hautecoeur, *Littérature et peinture en France*, Paris, 1942 / A. Hoeber, *The Barbizon Painters*, Philadelphia, 1915 / S. Hunter, *Modern French Painting 1855-1956*, New York, 1956 / R. Huyghe, *French Painting: Contemporaries*, Paris, New York, 1939 / P. Lavedan, *French Architecture*, Paris, 1944; Baltimore, 1956 / Luc-Benoist, *La sculpture française*, Paris, 1945 / R. Nacenta, *School of Paris*, Greenwich, Conn., 1960 / J. Rewald, *The History of Impressionism*, New York, 1946, 1961 / J. Rewald, *Post-Impressionism from Van Gogh to Gauguin*, New York, 1956, 1962 / R. Schneider, *L'art français, XIXe siècle*, Paris, 1929 / L. Venturi, *Impressionists and Symbolists*, New York, 1950 / R. H. Wilenski, *Modern French Painters*, New York, 1940, 1945.

GERMANY, HOLLAND, BELGIUM, SPAIN, PORTUGAL, and ELSEWHERE: A. Calzada, *Historia de la arquitectura española*, Barcelona, 1933 / F. Fosca, *Histoire de la peinture suisse*, Geneva, 1945 / H. Gotlib, *Polish Painting*, London, 1942 / A. Giefer, et al., *Planen und Bauen in neuen Deutschlands*, Cologne, 1960 / W. Gropius (ed.), *Bauhaus: 1919-1928*, Boston, 1938, 1959 / F. Haack, *Die Kunst des XIX Jahrhunderts*, Esslingen a.N., 1922 / P. Haesaerts, *Histoire de la peinture moderne en Flandre*, Brussels, 1960 / G. Händler, *German Painting in Our Time*, Berlin, 1956 / F. M. Huebner, *Die Neue Malerei in Holland*, Leipzig, 1921 / H. L. C. Jaffé, *De Stijl, 1917-1931*, London, 1956 / E. Lambert, *L'Art en Espagne et au Portugal*, Paris, 1945 / J. Lassaigne, *Spanish Painting from Velásquez to Picasso*, Geneva, 1952 / K. Millech, *Danske arkitektur strømninger*, Copenhagen, 1951 / B. S. Myers, *The German Expressionists*, New York, 1957 / G. E. Kidder Smith, *Sweden Builds*, London, 1950 / G. E. Kidder Smith, *Switzerland Builds*, London, 1950 / H. M. Wingler, *Das Bauhaus, 1919-1933*, Cologne, 1962.

ITALY: G. Ballo, *Modern Italian Painting*, New York, 1958 / C. Carro, *Il Rinnovamento delle arte in Italia*, Milan, 1945 / R. Carrieri, *Avant-garde Painting and Sculpture*, Milan, 1955 / E. Lavagnino, *L'Arte moderna*, Torino, 1956 / A. Melani, *L'architettura nel Secolo XIX*, Milan, 1899 / U. Ojetti, *La Pittura italiana dell'Ottocento*, Milan, 1929 / C. Pagani, *Italy's Architecture Today*, Milan, 1955 / G. E. Kidder Smith, *Italy Builds*, New York, 1955 / J. C. Taylor, *Futurism*, New York, 1961 / A. R. Willard, *History of Modern Italian Art*, New York, 1900.

RUSSIA: A. Benois, *The Russian School of Painting*, New York, 1916 / C. Gray, *The Great Experiment, Russian Art 1863-1922*, New York, 1962 / G. H. Hamilton, *Art and Architecture of Russia*, Baltimore, 1954 / G. K. Loukomski, *History of Modern Russian Painting*, London, 1945 / L. Réau, *L'Art Russe, Vol. 2*, Paris, 1922 / T. T. Rice, *Russian Art*, West Drayton, Middlesex, 1949 / A. Voyce, *Russian Architecture*, New York, 1948.

MONOGRAPHS

C. Giedion-Welcker, JEAN ARP, New York, 1957 / C. Saunier, BARYE, Paris, 1925 / G. W. Eggers, GEORGE BELLOWS, New York, 1931 / A. Blunt, THE ART OF WILLIAM BLAKE, New York, 1959 / G. C. Argan, UMBERTO BOCCIONI, Rome, 1953 / M. Tinti, LORENZO BARTOLINI, Rome, 1936 / J. Rewald, PIERRE BONNARD, New York, 1948 / G. Varenne, BOURDELLE PAR LUI-MEME, Paris, 1937 / G. Cahen, EUGENE BOUDIN, Paris, 1900 / C. Giedion-Welcker, CONSTANTIN BRANCUSI, Basel, 1958 / H. R. Hope, GEORGES BRAQUE, New York, 1949 / J. J. Sweeney, ALEXANDER CALDER, New York, 1951 / E. Bassi, CANOVA, Bergamo, 1952 / E. Chesneau, LE STATUAIRE J. B. CARPEAUX, Paris, 1880 / M. Breuning, MARY CASSATT, New York, 1944 / L. Venturi, CEZANNE, SON ART, SON OEUVRE, Paris, 1936 / M. Schapiro, PAUL CEZANNE, New York, 1952 / F. Meyer, MARC CHAGALL, Cologne, 1961 / L. Bénédicte, THEODORE CHASSERIAU, Paris, 1931 / J. T. Soby, GIORGIO DE CHIRICO, New York, 1955 / C. R. Leslie, MEMOIRS OF THE LIFE OF JOHN CONSTABLE, 1843, 1937 / A. Robaut, L'OEUVRE DE COROT, Paris, 1905 / G. Riat, GUSTAVE COURBET, PEINTRE, Paris, 1906 / G. Mack, GUSTAVE COURBET, New York, 1951 / J. T. Soby, SALVADOR DALI, New York, 1946 / J. David, LE PEINTRE LOUIS DAVID, Paris, 1880 / K. Holma, DAVID, Paris, 1940 / H. Jouin, DAVID D'ANGERS, Paris, 1878 / E. C. Goossen, STUART DAVIS, New York, 1959 / E. Klossowski, HONORE DAUMIER, Munich, 1923 / J. Adhémar, HONORE DAUMIER, New York, Basel, 1954 / P. A. Lemoisne, DEGAS ET SON OEUVRE, Paris, 1946-49 / D. C. Rich, DEGAS, New York, 1951 / R. Huyghe, DELACROIX, New York, Paris, 1955 / E. Delacroix, JOURNAL (Joubin ed.) Paris, 1932. (W. Pach trans. New York, 1937) / G. Hilaire, DERAIN, Geneva, 1959 / J. Lassaigne, DUFY, Geneva, 1954 / L. Goodrich, THOMAS EAKINS, New York, 1933 / J. Prevost, EIFFEL, Paris, 1929 / J. Epstein, AN AUTOBIOGRAPHY, New York, 1955 / L. Tannenbaum, JAMES ENSOR, New York, 1951 / P. Waldberg, MAX ERNST, Paris, 1958 / W. Wolfradt, CASPAR DAVID FRIEDRICH, Berlin, 1924 / R. J. Goldwater, GAUGUIN, New York, 1957 / H. R. Hitchcock, GAUDI, New York, 1957 / C. Clément, GERICAULT, 3rd ed., Paris, 1879 / K. Berger, GERICAULT AND HIS WORK, Lawrence, 1955 / A. L. Mayer, FRANCISCO DE GOYA, Munich, 1923, London, 1924 / J. López-Rey, GOYA'S CAPRICHOS, Princeton, 1953 / D. H. Kahnweiler, JUAN GRIS, Paris, New York, 1947 / S. Giedion, WALTER GROPIUS, New York, London, 1954 / J. Tripier Le Franc, BARON GROS, Paris, 1880 / L. Goodrich, WINSLOW HOMER, New York, 1944 / N. Schlenoff, INGRES, SES SOURCES LITTERAIRES, Paris, 1956 / G. Wildenstein, INGRES, London, Paris, 1954 / E. McClausland, GEORGE INNESS, New York, 1946 / E. Moreau-Nélaton, JONGKIND, Paris, 1918 / W. Grohmann, KANDINSKY, LIFE AND WORK, New York, 1958 / W. Grohmann, PAUL KLEE, New York, 1954 / H. M. Wingler, OSKAR KOKOSCHKA, Salzburg, 1958 / W.

Armstrong, SIR THOMAS LAWRENCE, London, 1913 / M. Raval and J. C. Moreux, C. N. LEDOUX, Paris, 1945 / K. Kuh, LEGER, Urbana, 1953 / W. Boesiger, LE CORBUSIER & PIERRE JEANNERET, Zurich, 1937-57 / I. Patai, ENCOUNTERS, THE LIFE OF JACQUES LIPCHITZ, New York, 1961 / T. Howarth, CHARLES RENNIE MACKINTOSH, London, 1952 / J. Cladel, MAILLOL, Paris, 1937 / C. L. Ragghianti, GIACOMO MANZU, SCULPTOR, Milan, 1957 / M. Helm, JOHN MARIN, Boston, 1948 / A. Tabarant, MANET ET SES OEUVRES, Paris, 1947 / S. L. Faison, MANET, New York, 1953 / J. Cartwright, JEAN FRANCOIS MILLET, New York, 1902 / P. Johnson, MIES VAN DER ROHE, New York, 1953 / M. Seuphor, PIET MONDRIAN, New York, 1956 / A. H. Barr Jr., MATISSE, HIS ART AND HIS PUBLIC, New York, 1951 / J. Dupin, MIRO, New York, 1962 / W. Seitz, CLAUDE MONET, New York, 1960 / H. Read, HENRY MOORE, London, 1955-57 / A. Salmon, MODIGLIANI, A MEMOIR, Paris, 1957, New York, 1961 / F. B. Deknatel, EDVARD MUNCH, Boston, 1950 / J. N. Summerson, JOHN NASH, London, 1935 / G. C. Argan, PIERLUIGI NERVI, Milan, 1955 / A. Reed, OROZCO, New York, 1956 / E. Rogers, AUGUSTE PERRET, Milan, 1955 / R. Massat, PEVSNER ET LE CONSTRUCTIVISME, Paris, 1956 / C. Zervos, PABLO PICASSO, OEUVRES, Paris, 1932- / A. H. Barr, Jr., PICASSO, FIFTY YEARS OF HIS ART, New York, 1946 / L. R. Pissarro and L. Venturi, CAMILLE PISSARRO, Paris, 1939 / B. Robertson, JACKSON POLLOCK, New York, 1960 / H. H. Rhys, MAURICE PRENDERGAST, Harvard, 1960 / R. Bacou, ODILON REDON, Geneva, 1956 / J. Renoir, RENOIR, MY FATHER, Boston, 1962 / A. Vollard, RENOIR, Paris, 1919, New York, 1925 / W. Armstrong, SIR HENRY RAEBURN, London, 1901 / H. R. Hitchcock, THE ARCHITECTURE OF H. H. RICHARDSON AND HIS TIMES, New York, 1936 / J. Cladel, RODIN, Paris, 1936; New York, 1937 / A. Elsen, RODIN, New York, 1963 / H. C. Marillier, D. G. ROSSETTI, London, 1899 / P. Courthion, GEORGES ROUAULT, New York, 1962 / A. Temko, EERO SAARINEN, New York, 1962 / H. Dorra and J. Rewald, SEURAT, Paris, 1959 / J. T. Soby, BEN SHAHN, W. Drayton, 1947 / F. Daulte, ALFRED SISLEY, Paris, 1959 / J. N. Summerson, SIR JOHN SOANE, London, 1952 / A. Griesebach, KARL FRIEDRICH SCHINKEL, Leipzig, 1924 / W. T. Whitley, GILBERT STUART, Harvard, 1932 / D. C. Rich, HENRI ROUSSEAU, New York, 1946 / H. Morrison, LOUIS SULLIVAN, New York, 1952 / M. Joyant, H. DE TOULOUSE-LAUTREC, Paris, 1926-27 / D. Cooper, TOULOUSE-LAUTREC, New York, 1952 / A. J. Finberg, THE LIFE OF J. M. W. TURNER, Oxford, 1939 / J. B. de La Faille, VAN GOGH, Paris, New York, 1939 / M. Schapiro, VAN GOGH, New York, 1950 / J. P. Crespelle, VLAMINCK, Paris, 1958 / A. C. Richie, EDOUARD VUILLARD, New York, 1954 / E. R. and J. Pennell, THE LIFE OF JAMES MC NEILL WHISTLER, London, 1908, New York, 1920 / F. Gutheim (ed.) FRANK LLOYD WRIGHT ON ARCHITECTURE, New York, 1941.

INDEX

Artists, sculptors, architects and craftsmen are shown in regular type and art movements are in *italics*.